# For Richer, Not Poorer

# For Richer, Not Poorer

## THE NEWLYWEDS' FINANCIAL SURVIVAL GUIDE

Deborah A. Wilburn

A PERIGEE BOOK

**THE BERKLEY PUBLISHING GROUP**
**Published by the Penguin Group**
**Penguin Group (USA) Inc.**
**375 Hudson Street, New York, New York 10014, USA**
Penguin Group (Canada), 10 Alcorn Avenue, Toronto, Ontario M4V 3B2, Canada
(a division of Pearson Penguin Canada Inc.)
Penguin Books Ltd., 80 Strand, London WC2R 0RL, England
Penguin Group Ireland, 25 St. Stephen's Green, Dublin 2, Ireland (a division of Penguin Books Ltd.)
Penguin Group (Australia), 250 Camberwell Road, Camberwell, Victoria 3124, Australia
(a division of Pearson Australia Group Pty. Ltd.)
Penguin Books India Pvt. Ltd., 11 Community Centre, Panchsheel Park, New Delhi—110 017, India
Penguin Group (NZ), Cnr. Airborne and Rosedale Roads, Albany, Auckland 1310, New Zealand
(a division of Pearson New Zealand Ltd.)
Penguin Books (South Africa) (Pty.) Ltd., 24 Sturdee Avenue, Rosebank, Johannesburg 2196,
South Africa

Penguin Books Ltd., Registered Offices: 80 Strand, London WC2R 0RL, England

PRINTING HISTORY
Perigee trade paperback edition / June 2005

ISBN: 0-399-53153-X

PERIGEE is a registered trademark of Penguin Group (USA) Inc.
The "P" design is a trademark belonging to Penguin Group (USA) Inc.

Library of Congress Cataloging-in-Publication Data

Wilburn, Deborah A., 1954–
        For richer, not poorer : the newlyweds' financial survival guide / by Deborah A. Wilburn.
            p. cm.
        ISBN 0-399-53153-X
        1. Married people—Finance, Personal. 2. Finance, Personal. I. Title.

    HG179.W5267 2005
    332.024'0086'55—dc22                                                2005045801

PRINTED IN THE UNITED STATES OF AMERICA

10  9  8  7  6  5  4  3  2  1

*For Rich and Cary,*
*the fabulous men in my life.*

# Contents

# Acknowledgments

I would like to thank the many experts who generously gave of their time and knowledge throughout the research phase of this project. It would not have been possible for me to complete this book without their input and, in some cases, review of the manuscript. I would especially like to thank Andrew Altfest of L. J. Altfest & Co., Inc.; Steven P. Copeland, CFP, Safe Harbor Financial Planning; Joseph R. Romano, CFP, president, Romano Brothers & Co.; Bonnie Ashby Hughes, CFP, A&H Financial Planning and Education, Inc.; Greg McGraime, CFP, ChFC, vice president, JP Morgan Chase Bank; Shashin G. Shah, CFP, Financial Design Group; Victoria Collins, Ph.D., CFP, The Keller Group Investment Management, Inc.; Larina Kase, Psy.D., MBA, president, Performance and Success Coaching, LLC; Bill Cochran, marriage coach in Derwood, Maryland; Joan Atwood, Ph.D., director of Marriage and Family Therapy programs, Hofstra University; Olivia Mellan, money psychologist, Olivia Mellan & Associates, Inc.; Marsha G. LePhew, CPA, PC; Warren Racusin, senior estate planning partner, McElroy, Deutsch, Mulvaney & Carpenter; Diane Giarratano, director of education for NovaDebt; Ginita Wall, cofounder, Women's Institute for Financial Education; John Vaccaro, chief marketing officer, Hartford Financial Services Group; Carol Harnett, national practice leader, Hartford Financial Services Group; Jeanne Salvatore, vice president, consumer affairs, Insurance Information Institute; Betty Messman, housing manager, Credit Counseling Network, Fort Worth, Texas; Catherine Williams, vice president, financial literacy, Money Management International; Joe Conyard, mortgage broker, GMAC; Dorcas Helfant, former president, National Association of Realtors, Realtor with Coldwell Banker; Bob Armbruster, president, National Association of Mortgage Brokers, president, Armbruster Mortgage Services; Doug Charney, president, The Charney Investment Group; Eva Rosenberg, MBA, EA; John Ford, chief privacy officer, Equifax; Ken McEldowney, executive director, Consumer Action; and Robert J. Nachshin, certified specialist in Family Law, Nachshin & Weston.

Thank you, too, to the brides who opened up so willingly about their finances and the emotional issues that surround money. It is my wish that your marriages will thrive in every way possible.

I am very fortunate to count as friends very gifted writers and editors who have offered invaluable support and feedback, particularly Melissa Stanton, Caitlin Kelly and Nicola Bridges. Special thanks go to Gini Kopecky Wallace, for her always incisive editorial comments, and for her constant encouragement. I also owe a debt of gratitude to Pam Young, whose kind and generous support was invaluable.

Finally, I must thank my husband, Rich, for his steadfast love and support and for putting up with my many evenings and weekends spent in front of the computer. If anyone ever tells you that being a writer is glamorous, don't believe them!

# Introduction

Brides today are savvier than ever. They know how to find a bargain bridal gown, how to cut the cost of wedding flowers and which smart questions to ask a photographer. However, something they don't always know how to do—or are reluctant to do—is to talk in-depth to their fiancé about money. It's relatively easy to cover the basics: How much will we spend on the wedding? How much do we each bring home each week? But many couples are hesitant to delve deeper than that. They may not be sure how much debt their partner is carrying, or if their fiancé contributes to a 401(k) plan and, if so, how much money is in it. Money can be a sticky subject, one we don't necessarily want to broach. Why? Because doing so just doesn't seem romantic— after all, we're marrying for love, not money, right?

While that's true, the fact remains that marriage is a merger not only of your lives but of your finances. For better or worse, you are becoming business partners in the running of your household and family, and your fortunes will now rise and fall together. The sooner you provide full disclosure about your finances, and learn to talk to each other about money in a way that moves you toward your shared goals, the better.

The purpose of this book is twofold: First, to give you a firm grounding in the basics of personal finance so that you can pour that all-important foundation for a lifetime of financial security and prosperity. For example, should you invest in a 401(k) or an IRA? How much? When should you buy a house? What type of mortgage should you get? Which should you pay off first: credit card debt or student loans? What is the best way of managing your credit cards so that your credit rating remains high? How can you repair a poor credit score? Do you need wills? These are just some of the basic questions that will be answered. Second, my intent is to help you learn how to have constructive money conversations now, and in the future, to avoid some of the costly problems and misunderstandings that a lack of communication— or negative communication (also called arguments!)—can bring about. While I primarily address brides, any husbands who happen to be reading this book can obviously apply these concepts as well.

As a personal finance writer, I've been a regular contributor to *Modern Bride,* and to *Elegant Bride,* where I am a contributing editor, helping brides-to-be and their future spouses make smart financial choices as they prepare for married life. In this capacity and during the research of this book, I have had the privilege of interviewing some of the top financial professionals in the country, including certified financial planners, investment advisors, money psychologists and experts on everything from buying insurance to investing in 401(k) plans—all geared to steer you in the right direction while leaving out the extraneous stuff you don't need to deal with right now (like long-term-care insurance).

# For Richer, Not Poorer

# 1. You're Engaged! Time to Get Real with Yourself and Your Finances

So far, you've been managing money on your own since, when? College? High school? You've developed your own system for paying bills; you've come up with your own budget, however loosely you want to define the term. You know if you're the type who uses credit cards to buy things you can't really afford (Jimmy Choo shoes, anyone?) or if you're great at socking away every spare dime. And if you don't know these things about yourself, now is a good time to take a mini self-inventory on your relationship with money: What are you bringing to your marital relationship when it comes to managing your cash? What are your strengths and weaknesses? Are you laidback about money, or anxious? Are you a spender or saver? Do you often, sometimes or never balance your checkbook? How might your money management style help or hinder you from reaching money goals, such as buying a house or a new car or saving for a baby? How will your style mesh with that of your Future Husband (FH)? (You'll learn more about that in chapter 2.)

You need to get real with yourself because you'll need to get real with your FH as well (and he with you, with the help of the handy exercises and worksheets in this book). The point is, you're not going it alone anymore—one of the great benefits of marriage. You're becoming a part of a team, creating a business partnership. No longer Me, Inc., soon you'll become Mr. and Mrs. So and So, Inc. And the more you know about yourselves and each other—the focus here being on finances—the better you'll be able to make your new partnership flourish and grow. In the spirit, then, of further Knowing Thyself . . .

## Show Me Yours and I'll Show You Mine (Balance Sheet, That Is)

A balance sheet is simply a list of all of your assets (money and other valuables that you own) and liabilities (debt). By subtracting your liabilities from your assets, you'll have your net worth. It's important for you and your FH to exchange balance sheets so you'll know what you're each starting out with. You can then better devise an accurate joint spending plan to build on your assets and reach your goals.

This is also a good time to come clean on anything from your financial past that you so far may have hesitated to reveal in your relationship. Sometimes people feel nervous about letting their future spouse know how much debt they have, or what they have spent or like to spend their money on, or, for example, that they had a problem when they fell behind on taxes and had their wages garnished. But it's better to get everything on the table now. You'll find that withholding anything takes up more psychic energy than it's worth. And, as we'll see in the following section on money secrets, coming clean often doesn't have as devastating an effect on the relationship as you might imagine it will. As you tackle the first worksheet and lay out the truth about your finances, lovingly request that your FH do the same.

# BALANCE SHEET

## (HER COPY)

## INCOME

Your salary or projected annual income, if self-employed $_____

Anticipated bonuses . . . . . . . . . . . . . . . . . . . . . . . . . . . . $_____

Commissions . . . . . : . . . . . . . . . . . . . . . . . . . . . . . . . $_____

## ASSETS (What you own)

### Cash and cash equivalents

*Note the balances in each of the following accounts:*

Cash in checking account . . . . . . . . . . . . . . . . . $_____

Cash in savings/money market accounts . . . . . . . $_____

Certificates of Deposit (CDs) . . . . . . . . . . . . . . . $_____

Savings bonds . . . . . . . . . . . . . . . . . . . . . . . . . $_____

Life insurance cash value . . . . . . . . . . . . . . . . . $_____

Money owed you . . . . . . . . . . . . . . . . . . . . . . . $_____

### Personal property

*State the estimated current market value for each item:*

Home or apartment . . . . . . . . . . . . . . . . . . . . . . $_____

Other real estate . . . . . . . . . . . . . . . . . . . . . . . . $_____

Car(s) . . . . . . . . . . . . . . . . . . . . . . . . . . . . . . . $_____

Jewelry, furs . . . . . . . . . . . . . . . . . . . . . . . . . . . $_____

Boat . . . . . . . . . . . . . . . . . . . . . . . . . . . . . . . . . $_____

Art, antiques . . . . . . . . . . . . . . . . . . . . . . . . . . . $_____

Other . . . . . . . . . . . . . . . . . . . . . . . . . . . . . . . . $_____

**Investments**

*Note the balances in each of the following accounts:*

401(k) . . . . . . . . . . . . . . . . . . . . . . . . . . . . . . . . $_____

IRA, Roth IRA . . . . . . . . . . . . . . . . . . . . . . . . . . $_____

Keogh, SEP IRA . . . . . . . . . . . . . . . . . . . . . . . . $_____

Mutual funds . . . . . . . . . . . . . . . . . . . . . . . . . . . $_____

Stocks, bonds, government securities . . . . . . . . . $_____

Equity in your own business . . . . . . . . . . . . . . . . $_____

Other . . . . . . . . . . . . . . . . . . . . . . . . . . . . . . . . . $_____

**TOTAL ASSETS** . . . . . . . . . . . . . . . . . . . . . . . . . . $_____

(Add all of the above except Income)


**LIABILITIES** (What you owe)

**Current bills outstanding**

(rent, utilities, insurance premiums, etc.) . . . . . . . . $_____

**Credit card debt** (total of all cards) . . . . . . . . . . . . . . . . .$_____

Interest rate(s) (Give range if more than one credit card): _____%

**Mortgage** . . . . . Balance due: $_____ Interest rate: _____%

**Auto loan** . . . . . Balance due: $_____ Interest rate: _____%

**Student loan(s)** Balance due: $_____ Interest rate: _____%

(If more than one loan, add them up, and give range of interest rates)

**401(k) loan** . . . . . . . . . . . . . . . . . . . . . . . . . . . . . . . $_____

**Other loans** . . . . . . . . . . . . . . . . . . . . . . . . . . . . . . . $_____


**NET WORTH** . . . . . . . . . . . . . . . . . . . . . . . . . . . . . . $_____

(Subtract Liabilities from Assets)

# BALANCE SHEET

## (HIS COPY)

## INCOME

Your salary or projected annual income, if self-employed $_____

Anticipated bonuses ............................. $_____

Commissions ................................. $_____

## ASSETS (What you own)

### Cash and cash equivalents

*Note the balances in each of the following accounts:*

Cash in checking account ................... $_____

Cash in savings/money market accounts ....... $_____

Certificates of Deposit (CDs) ................ $_____

Savings bonds ........................... $_____

Life insurance cash value ................... $_____

Money owed you .......................... $_____

### Personal Property

*State the estimated current market value for each item:*

Home or apartment ........................ $_____

Other real estate .......................... $_____

Car(s) ................................... $_____

Jewelry, furs ............................. $_____

Boat .................................... $_____

Art, antiques ............................. $_____

Other ................................... $_____

## Investments

*Note the balances in each of the following accounts:*

401(k) . . . . . . . . . . . . . . . . . . . . . . . . . . . . . . . . . . $_____

IRA, Roth IRA . . . . . . . . . . . . . . . . . . . . . . . . . . . $_____

Keogh, SEP IRA . . . . . . . . . . . . . . . . . . . . . . . . . . $_____

Mutual funds . . . . . . . . . . . . . . . . . . . . . . . . . . . . . $_____

Stocks, bonds, government securities . . . . . . . . . $_____

Equity in your own business . . . . . . . . . . . . . . . . . $_____

Other . . . . . . . . . . . . . . . . . . . . . . . . . . . . . . . . . . . $_____

## TOTAL ASSETS . . . . . . . . . . . . . . . . . . . . . . . . . . . . $_____

(Add all of the above except Income)


## LIABILITIES (What you owe)

### Current bills outstanding

(rent, utilities,insurance premiums, etc.) . . . . . . . . $_____

**Credit card debt** (total of all cards) . . . . . . . . . . . . . . . . .$_____

Interest rate(s) (Give range if more than one credit card): _____%

**Mortgage** . . . . . Balance due: $_____ Interest rate: _____%

**Auto loan** . . . . . Balance due: $_____ Interest rate: _____%

**Student loan(s)** Balance due: $_____ Interest rate: _____%

(If more than one loan, add them up, and give range of interest rates)

**401(k) loan** . . . . . . . . . . . . . . . . . . . . . . . . . . . . . . . . . $_____

**Other loans** . . . . . . . . . . . . . . . . . . . . . . . . . . . . . . . . . $_____


## NET WORTH . . . . . . . . . . . . . . . . . . . . . . . . . . . . . . . . $_____

(Subtract Liabilities from Assets)

Looking over your balance sheets not only gives you an overview of each other's finances, it also starts to give you some understanding of how you each handle money. Here's what to look for: amount of debt. How high is it? Where does it come from—credit cards, student loans or . . . ? Assets. If he has a large balance in one or more accounts, you ought to ask where it came from. Is it from savings? An inheritance? You'll also want to ask your FH what plans he has for the money. Will the two of you be utilizing it together, or will he keep it as a separate asset? Does he have savings in any retirement accounts? If not, ask him about that. Perhaps he hasn't been eligible for any such account at work, it wasn't available or he didn't think it was important to save for that purpose. Try using these worksheets as a springboard for discussion about what your money priorities have been to this point and how you anticipate that they will change. Ideally, the balance sheets will also start to give you some ideas on what types of money goals you'll want to work toward after marriage (further discussed in chapter 5).

## We Have No (Money) Secrets

Have you each told all on your worksheets? Nothing can do more harm to a sense of trust and respect between partners than a withheld secret coming to light, as they all eventually do. While it's never our intent to damage a relationship, that is the risk we take by withholding something about our financial background. Think of it this way: How would you feel if, after the wedding, you discovered that your now Darling Husband (DH) "forgot" to tell you about something significant, such as a bankruptcy that is still part of his credit record? This is no trivial matter, because it would certainly affect your ability to secure a mortgage at the most favorable interest rates, if you could get one at all (assuming you needed both incomes to qualify). When such information is withheld, it's natural to feel deceived and to legit-imately wonder if there are other secrets you don't know about.

Danielle, thirty-one, a writer who lives in New York City, was ex-tremely reluctant to tell her husband, Oren, thirty-three, an account-ant, the amount of debt she had before their wedding in August 2003. She had several thousand dollars in credit card debt and much more in graduate school student loans. "My dad helped me out a lot over the years," she says. "He paid my undergrad student loans, and often he'd pay my credit card bills." But when her father went through a messy second divorce, the money dried up.

"Oren came from nothing and he's always been a saver," says Danielle. "He knew I had debt, but he didn't know the numbers. When I finally did tell him, he couldn't believe I allowed myself to owe money in any way, shape or form. I was afraid he wouldn't marry me. I was getting his plusses and he was getting my minuses." But Oren wasn't going to let debt stop him from marrying the woman he loved.

He requested that Danielle pay off her credit card debt before the wedding, which she did. They had moved in together a year before their planned wedding date, and the fact that they were sharing living expenses made it easier for her to pay what she owed. At times he was too upset to even talk about the student loans, so she just kept mak-ing her minimum monthly payments. Danielle notes that after being married for a year, they were finally able to discuss her education debt without it turning into an argument. They decided to try to re-tire the debt more aggressively, and found the funds to "pay off a nice chunk," she says.

In Danielle's case, she thought her fiancé would leave her after she spilled. While Oren certainly wasn't happy about the debt, instead of leaving, he worked with her to find a way to address the situation head-on.

And therein lies the key. If, in telling your FH about some nasty financial secret, you also state (and, if possible, demonstrate) your intent to reform, it will make it much easier to get beyond any initial negative reaction and move ahead. Obviously, if your FH has something to spill, you're apt to be a lot more understanding about the problem if, likewise, he is on the path to reform.

Julie, thirty-four, a publications secretary in Milwaukee, Wisconsin, has been married to John, thirty-five, a store manager, for one-and-a-half years. Julie says that when they went into "full disclosure" mode before they married, John was surprised to find out that she had had a bankruptcy in her past. "Long story, bad situation," sums up Julie. She says she did feel guilty telling him about it, knowing how he felt about debt in general (he had none). "Actually, he was kind of angry," she says. "He's worked hard to keep his credit rating good. It took time but he's made his peace with my situation." In the aftermath of her money troubles, she says she avoids credit cards as much as possible. "But because I'm rebuilding my credit, I do charge small things every month to reestablish a record of making payments on time," she says.

Clearly, revealing past money mistakes isn't something anyone relishes. No one wants to appear in an unfavorable light, and there is always a fear of rejection, no matter how unfounded. But, as the saying goes, and as Danielle and Julie each discovered, love conquers all. If you have a money secret to reveal, think of the relief you'll feel, as they did, to finally get it off your chest. Indeed, going through this exercise might be the first instance in which your partner has a chance to show you he will be there for you, "for better or for worse." If you remain hesitant to have this conversation, you might consider going for premarital counseling. This can offer a safe place for you to bring up the topic, knowing a counselor is there to help the two of you talk through any issues. If the worst should happen and he calls it quits, it's highly likely that this wasn't the only thing to make him hesitate. Wouldn't you rather know now, rather than later, if his heart isn't fully committed to you?

We have been talking about your revealing any money secret you might have kept, but obviously you'll want to question your fiancé if there is something in his money past that doesn't seem to add up. It's only fair that you each have all your cards on the table. For example, has he noted on his balance sheet a monthly payment and you don't understand what it's for? Ask him. While some of the questions we need to ask may be difficult—most of us are not used to talking freely about money—having these conversations can actually bring the two of you closer as you truly bare all. Of course, you and your FH may not feel compelled to share every thought and feeling you have—after all, a bit of mystery is sexy. But when it comes to finances, it is important to be open and honest. Then you can plan together in confidence that you have the whole picture and there will be no surprises. That said, you're ready to dig one level deeper into your financial pasts.

## Order Your Credit Histories and FICO Scores

Were you under the impression that you and your FH are finished making disclosures? Sorry, but there's one more to go! You have probably been talking about buying a house or a new car, or making some other major purchase in the not-too-distant future. That's why, in addition to exchanging balance sheets, you'll each want to get copies of your credit reports and FICO scores from the three major credit reporting agencies. A FICO score uses a mathematical formula to "summarize" your credit history in the form of a number. It is used to determine how much of a credit risk you represent to lenders. Reviewing your reports will give you a heads-up on any inaccuracies, out-of-date information or debts that could impact your score (for example, that unpaid cable bill from your last apartment). It is a good idea for you and your FH to exchange reports to see how your collective credit might look to a bank or other lender. Thanks to an amendment to the Fair Credit Reporting Act, you are now entitled to a free copy of your report from each of the three major credit reporting agencies once a year. This entitlement is being rolled out across the country from west to east, beginning December 1, 2004, and ending September 1, 2005. You can request a free copy of your report from each of the three major credit reporting agencies (Equifax, Transunion and Experian) once every twelve months by phone, mail or on the Internet. To find out when it's available in your state and to order your report online, go to www.AnnualCreditReport.com. You may also call 1-877-322-8228 or write to Annual Credit Report Request Service, P.O. Box 105281, Atlanta, Georgia, 30348-5283 to order your free copy. For more information regarding credit reports and your rights as a consumer, go to the Federal Trade Commission's website (www.ftc.gov). To get information about disputing or correcting information in your report contact the agency that issued it:

**Equifax:** www.equifax.com or call 800-685-1111
**Transunion:** www.transunion.com or call 800-916-8800
**Experian:** www.experian.com or call 888-397-3742

You are also entitled to a free copy of your report if you are ever turned down for credit, insurance or employment, are unemployed and you plan to look for a job within 60 days or are a victim of identity theft. Otherwise you may be charged up to $9.95 for another copy of your report within the twelve-month period.

You actually have three FICO scores, generated from the information gathered by each of the three major credit reporting agencies. (The data in your file varies from agency to agency, which is why you need to check it with all three.) Since the FICO score is compiled by Fair Isaac Corporation, a separate company, it doesn't come with your credit report and must be bought separately. You can buy your scores from Fair Isaacs's site (www.myfico.com) or from any one of the three credit reporting agencies.

## Fun Facts About Your FICO Score

FICO scores range between 300 and 850, with 720 being the median score (half are above that score and half are below it). While lenders use more than one tool in determining credit worthiness (for example, your income and length of time on the job, or how much money you have in the bank), those who score in the 700+ range usually qualify for the best rates the lender can offer. Ever wonder how the FICO algorithm weighs various aspects of your credit history in determining your score? Here are the five major factors and their level of importance:

Payment history: . . . . . . . . . . . . . . . . . . . . . . . .35%

How much you owe in total: . . . . . . . . . . . . . . .30%

Length of your credit history: . . . . . . . . . . . . . .15%

Your mix of credit
(i.e., credit cards, car loan, etc.): . . . . . . . . . .10%

New credit (number of recently opened
accounts and inquiries for new credit): . . . . .10%

How can you keep your score as high as possible? It's difficult to come up with any one set of hard-and-fast rules. (Read: FICO isn't about to give away any secrets that would allow consumers to crack their code.) Needless to say, scores are highly individualized, based on each person's particular financial history. For example, you might have a lot of credit cards, but that could be counterbalanced by your not having any recent inquiries on your record. Here are some general ways in which to maintain/improve your score:

- Pay your bills on time.

- Make sure your credit reports are accurate. There could be a mistake needlessly affecting your score.

- Don't run your cards up to the credit limit. If your cards are maxed out, stop charging and start paying them down. Potential lenders (a bank, a mortgage lender) want you to have access to credit, and they want to see you use it responsibly, but they don't want to see you living near the limit—it means you could miss a payment at any moment. Indeed, a FICO spokesperson says it would be advisable not to use more than 20 percent of available credit on your cards at any one time. You may think, 20 percent?! That's what I thought, anyway. Thing is, we may have gotten confused about the purpose of credit cards. They're not meant to function as installment loans, where it's understood that you carry a large balance over time. Credit cards are meant to be used for convenience—meaning, a short-term use of credit. Perhaps looking at it that way helps make sense of the fact that it can affect your score if your balances remain high over a long period of time. Note that while a FICO representative cautioned not to use more than 20 percent of your available credit, another credit expert mentioned 35 percent as the magic number you don't want to exceed. Either way, the faster you can pay off your balance the better off you'll be.

- The longer your credit account history, the better. Don't be in a rush to close out your oldest account, even if you're not using it. This is especially true if you're young and don't have a long credit history to begin with.

- Don't go willy-nilly applying for new credit, especially if you're on the verge of applying for a mortgage or car loan. Recent inquiries cause a short-term ding to your credit score. In addition, don't apply for more credit than you need. Try to avoid department store cards, even though they tend to give you 10 percent off all purchases on the day you open the account; they come with very high interest rates. If you charge more than you can afford each month, you'll pay dearly.

- It's a good idea to keep one or two credit cards, and to manage them responsibly. According to FICO, someone with no credit cards is a higher risk than someone who has managed credit responsibly.

- It will also help your score to have a mix of credit. Studies show that people with an assortment (credit cards, auto loan, mortgage) tend to be more responsible. In addition, the thinking goes that people tend to settle down once they buy a house.

## Prenups: Who Needs 'Em?

Prenuptial agreements were once considered the domain of the wealthy, but they have become increasingly common among the middle class, especially in second or third marriages when children are involved, or when couples bring individual assets, such as a home or a business, to the union. According to Robert J. Nachshin, a top attorney with Nachshin & Weston who specializes in family law in Los Angeles, everyone should have a prenuptial agreement, even young couples starting out. "The reason for a prenup isn't because you don't trust your mate, it's because you don't trust the courts and what they will do in the event of divorce. A prenup spells out exactly what will happen if you part ways, so there aren't any surprises."

As Nachshin and his partner, Scott N. Weston, write in their book, *I Do, You Do . . . But Just Sign Here*, everyone brings something of value into a marriage, even if it's simply one's talents and capabilities—"intellectual assets"—that could net them a significant income during the course of the marriage. How future proceeds are divvied up can be set in writing by you and your FH, with the hope and expectation that the document will never come into play. For example, if one spouse writes a book or starts a business, the prenuptial agreement can award the rights of the book to the writer and the business to the owner/operator. Without a prenuptial agreement, the royalties from the book or business would be marital property.

A prenup can also be helpful in terms of estate planning. You can each spell out how you would want your property/belongings/assets to be disbursed. For couples with few assets, a provision can be made requiring each of you to maintain a life insurance policy of a certain amount, naming each other as the beneficiary. That way, in the face of the unthinkable, the surviving spouse isn't left with a stack of bills and housing costs that are only affordable with two incomes.

In addition to detailing property disbursement and estate planning, prenups typically cover spousal support, personal conduct (believe it or not, there could be a stipulation about what happens if you gain too much weight or he watches too much football) and sunset provisions, which would nullify the agreement after a certain number of years. The only things that can't be dealt with in a prenup are child custody, visitation and child support of children, born or unborn.

If you have any questions about whether or not you need a prenup, it would be worthwhile to lay out a few bucks for a consultation with a family law attorney and have your concerns addressed. Admittedly, this isn't akin to a romantic picnic in the park, but neither is today's 50 percent divorce rate. Better to pack your parachute ahead of time than find yourself in a financial free fall if your marriage should end. When meeting with the lawyer, ask questions like, what would happen if I were to divorce after two years, five years, ten years? What would happen to the assets I bring into the marriage, such as retirement funds, property or other valuables? You may be surprised to learn that something you've assumed would always be yours could become community property after the wedding. Better to enter into the marriage being absolutely sure that you're marrying the right person—and with the peace of mind that you won't be financially devastated if things unexpectedly go awry.

Should you and your FH decide to go forward with a prenup, it's important to work with an attorney who specializes in family law and has experience in the delicate work of writing and negotiating prenups. You certainly don't want someone who is going to take an adversarial approach. Finally, it's important to have the document drawn up properly. Three things to remember are:

- You must completely disclose all assets and liabilities. If you hide anything about your finances the agreement could be invalidated.

- Each of you must have legal representation to advise you of your rights. Thus, you'll each retain an attorney, and decide between you which lawyer will provide the initial draft of the agreement. The other attorney will then review it and negotiate any points deemed necessary. This is an important step because a prenup excessively unfair to either party could be thrown out by the courts in the event of a divorce.

- Finally, start the process way in advance of the wedding date— at least six months ahead of time. You don't want your discussions to interfere with the other wedding preparations and celebration. In addition, a prenup that appears to have been signed under pressure—say, the night before the wedding!— could be invalidated.

## CHOOSING A LAWYER

It's always best to get referrals from family, friends and other professionals you work with, such as your accountant. Meet with a few attorneys before making your selection—it's an important decision not to be taken lightly. Here are some preliminary questions to ask:

1.  How many prenuptial agreements have you drafted? (You'll want someone who has drafted at least fifty.)

2.  How many have you negotiated?

3.  How many of your agreements have been contested in the event of a divorce?

4.  Do you know my fiancé's attorney? (You want lawyers who are neither too adversarial nor too chummy.)

Sometimes parents insist on a prenup when a family business or considerable wealth is involved. While this request isn't unusual, it can become a problem when parents get overly involved, trying to negotiate terms and insisting on approval of the agreement.

Several of the brides interviewed for this book at least broached the subject of a prenup with their fiancés—sometimes at the behest of friends. Beth is a New York City writer who married Steven, a filmmaker and teacher, in the spring of 2004. Beth said that she and Steven never discussed a prenup, even though they each brought assets to the union—she owns an apartment in Manhattan and has money in an IRA and mutual funds, and her husband's family owns several apartment buildings in Brooklyn. "My friends who are divorced all advised me to get a prenup, and I chose to ignore them,"

Beth says. She notes that both sets of parents have been married "forever." She and Steven don't anticipate any serious breakdowns in their relationship, given these strong role models.

Nina, thirty-five, is a secretary in Cleveland, Ohio. She and her husband, Brian, thirty-five, another filmmaker, have been married since August 2003. Even though neither brought a lot of assets into the marriage, Nina wanted a prenup. "I research everything," she says. "Everyone says you should have one. I have a will, too. It's better to be prepared." Nina points out that no one ever gets married thinking they'll get divorced, but people do. "I figured it would be something we'd put in a box but never use." But Brian didn't like the idea. "He felt it was too much like an escape route," Nina says. "He listened to my reasoning, but in the end he said if we're committed to doing this, nobody gets out easy." Nina dropped the idea.

Some brides are more insistent. "I'm a control freak," says Katrina, forty-seven. "And from watching my grandmother, who was married more than once, and my mother, who left when I was six, I saw that marriage doesn't necessarily last." When Katrina was about to marry Bill, forty-eight, twelve years ago, she requested a prenup. He didn't want one, but she said she wouldn't marry him without it. Bill relented.

"I was taught that it's important to protect what you have," she says. "I came into the marriage with antiques, jewelry, more than $100,000 in assets. He had a clarinet and a used car, but he also had a medical degree, which represents financial potential." Katrina says that having the prenup saved her from losing her apartment and family money when the couple's marriage did, unfortunately, come to an end due to his infidelity. The terms of her agreement spelled out that if either of them left their home, after thirty days it would mean they're separated. After the thirty days she was to be paid a lump sum of $10,000. "I figured I'd need $3,000 for lawyers, $3,000 for taxes and around $3,000 for expenses if I decided to move." In addition, she negotiated to receive $25,000 in alimony, to be paid out over two years (which was paid, although her ex extended the payment plan to three years). The document noted that she had paid the $65,000 down payment on their apartment, which she would get back if the apartment were ever sold.

Katrina says that while the prenup made it possible for her to stay afloat during the emotional upheaval she experienced after her husband left, she discovered, belatedly, that she'd made some costly omissions. "I never even thought about health insurance," she says. "It only cost him $40 a month to keep me on his plan, but he took me right off it and I had to buy my own policy." In addition, she says, he took the new, leased car, leaving her with a used one, which broke down a year later. "I didn't anticipate having to go into debt to buy a new car." Finally, there is the question of her apartment. "Both of our names are on the title," she notes. "Even though the prenup states that I'll get my down payment back, we didn't take his name off the title or specify whether or not he's entitled to any of the profits when the apartment is sold." Katrina is hoping that since his earnings are considerably higher than hers, he won't make it an issue of it since her money enabled them to buy the apartment in the first place.

## The Prenup "Alternative"

Perhaps the previous section has gotten you thinking—but you're still hesitant about going forward with a prenup. If you don't want to "go there," there is something you can do to at least establish what you owned at the time of the marriage: In a nutshell, **keep excellent records.** Ginita Wall, CFP, an expert on women and money and cofounder of the Women's Institute for Financial Education (www.wife.org), recommends that you hold on to your premarriage 401(k), IRA and mutual fund statements, including the one that arrived just before you got married. Trying to get this information later could be next to impossible. Mutual fund companies won't provide records going back more than six years, banks go out of business or merge, the company managing your 401(k) changes and no one has the old records. So keeping your statements before and at the time of marriage is step one. Step two is to **keep your separate property separate**—that is, keep the account in your own name, and don't use marital funds to add to these investments. (Note: Adding your spouse's name as the beneficiary on these accounts does not automatically make them community property.) You and your FH can then open new retirement accounts after the wedding. These accounts will be considered community property, since they will be funded with money earned during your marriage.

Careful record-keeping is also important when making a major purchase, such as a house. At least write down—and keep bank statements to back you up—who contributed how much of the house down payment, if the money comes from separate funds. (If you're saving for the house down payment together, you don't need to keep a special record of it.) For example, if you sold a condo you owned before you got married and will use those proceeds to eventually buy another home with your spouse, keep the money in a separate account until you're ready to go ahead with the purchase. That way there will be a paper trail of where the money came from. Does all of this sound paranoid and nutty? It will only if your relationship sails along smoothly for the next forty-plus years. In that case, you can have a good time burning these backup documents, which will be needlessly taking up closet space—and I sincerely hope that will be the case!

# 2. Money 'Tudes: His and Hers

In the previous chapter, you and your FH disclosed the basic facts and figures about your finances. In this chapter, we'll explore the psychological side of money—your background, beliefs and expectations, your wants, needs, and fears about the green stuff that sometimes seems to rule our lives. It's important to not only understand these things about yourself, so that you're not blindly ruled by perceptions and emotions, but to understand them about your partner. As you'll discover, the more you can recognize where he is coming from (and he, you) the easier it will be to make sense of why he says the things he says or wants to make certain money choices. By understanding and accepting each other for who you are, you can begin to work to some level of compromise in areas where there is disagreement.

You and your FH have undoubtedly had money discussions in the past, but you may not have had reason to delve too deeply into what makes your individual money personalities tick. The questions below offer a great opportunity to do just that. You'll not only learn about each other's money attitudes, but you'll gain a truer understanding of each other's values and lifestyle objectives. Having these talks is also beneficial because doing so gets you in the habit of talking about money—a habit I wish I'd gotten into much earlier in my own relationship. You may think, not talk about money? Who would have a problem with that? Financial advisors say it's not at all unusual for couples to abstain from talking about their financial situation for months or even years!

After nearly seven years of marriage, my husband, Rich, and I didn't have our most meaningful money conversations until after I started working on this book. Strange as it may sound coming from a financial writer, it didn't occur to me to talk about these things and it didn't occur to him either. Money is not something that was discussed in my family and his attitude was, What is there to discuss, beyond who pays which bills? We were both putting money into our 401(k)s, we'd saved for a house. What else was there? But I can tell you that had I gained a better understanding of my husband's background and beliefs, it could have saved a lot of headaches later on.

Let me give you an example. A few years after we were married, my husband announced quite out of the blue that he wanted to start an import business. During our honeymoon we had traveled to Italy and he, as an Italian-American, had a profound *Roots* moment of recognition in which he felt deeply connected to the people, the culture and the very land around us as we traveled through Rome, Florence and Venice. From that moment on (and unbeknownst to me, at first), it became his desire to develop a business that would somehow keep us connected to Italy and require us to spend time there. Now, I would be the last to complain about frequent trips to Italy, but visiting is one thing—trying to start a business revolving around all things Italian is quite another! In any case, over time he developed the idea that he wanted to import handmade furnishings—furniture, lighting, ceramics and other accessories for the home. He also decided that he would keep his overhead costs down by marketing his products directly to interior designers over the internet. Do interior designers shop on the internet? We didn't know. Was there a market for the kinds of products we were about to import? Didn't know that either. But he went forward and created a business importing the work of some of the finest craftsmen in Italy.

Although Rich did have an entrepreneurial background, having run his own PR agency, this was all very foreign to me. I was afraid that starting a business in an area that neither of us knew much about would ruin us financially. I was also all too familiar with the Small Business Administration's statistics indicating that 95 percent of all new businesses fail within the first five years. But at first I wasn't able to express my deepest fears to Rich. I wanted to be a supportive wife, and I was concerned about quashing his dream. Perhaps deep down I was even afraid that if I stood in his way it could mean the end of our relationship. Thus, in spite of my considerable misgivings, I didn't object as he charged forward into the unknown.

I didn't realize that giving him emotional support without paying any attention to my need for some degree of financial security would create a breeding ground for anger and resentment. The fallout from the business—which did bring us near the brink of financial ruin— created an unbelievable amount of stress in our marriage. The problem was that throughout the entire ordeal, we weren't talking to each other in ways that were helpful and constructive. My main focus of conversation had to do with money and where it would come from. But as the money in our account dwindled, he stonewalled every time I brought up what we were going to do to resolve the problem. He just wouldn't talk about it, frustrating me even more. Time and again he'd say, "I'll take care of it." I didn't believe him.

What I didn't find out until much later was that he blocked me out intentionally so that my "negativity" wouldn't interfere with him reaching his dream. He didn't want any "negative energy" interfering with his "positive energy." But he never told me that was how he viewed my attempts to discuss our situation. All I saw was stonewalling, which made me even more nuts and more "negative."

So, how could this have been avoided? Communication, communication, communication. When Rich and I went through some of the exercises in this book, I asked him how he envisioned making money when we first got married. He'd had a job as a marketing/PR executive for as long as I'd known him, so you can imagine my surprise when he told me that it was his idea all along to start another business! Now, I'm not saying this would have been a deal-breaker, but it would have been helpful for me to know going into our marriage that that is how he saw himself making his contribution. I wouldn't have been caught unaware, and I'd like to think that with a greater degree of understanding we could have talked through handling a start-up in a way that wouldn't have jeopardized our financial security. In the end, Rich found a new job, and we're steadily regaining financial ground. Meanwhile, our furnishings business is operating as a sideline, not costing us anything except the debt we're working to pay down.

My story has a happy ending because Rich and I have survived as a couple and come out on the other side, even though there were many times I thought of leaving. Why? Because the money stress was so intense *and* we weren't working as a team to resolve our difficulties. Taking some of my own advice, we are now—finally—talking about money, agreeing on mutual goals and focusing on what we each need to do to reach those goals. I offer this to you as a cautionary tale of how difficult life can become if you are not communicating with each other in this vital area.

## The Meaning of Money

What follows is a detailed series of questions geared to help you and your FH talk about your money backgrounds, philosophical approaches and lifestyle desires. Answer the questions separately, and then compare answers. As I discovered from going through the exercises with Rich, giving thoughtful consideration to these questions and discussing them can take time. To get the most from this exercise, you may want to sit down once a week for a few weeks and go through a few of the questions at each sitting. Chances are you'll be amazed about the new insights you'll gain about yourself—and each other!

1. Did your parents talk to you about money? If so, which one, or did both talk to you about it? Did they teach you the same things, or did they give contradictory messages? If they didn't talk to you about money, what did you learn just from observing them?

2. How much money did your family have? Were they wealthy, comfortably middle-class or was there never enough? How has this affected the way you view the world? For example, as a place of plenty? A place of struggle? Do you have a sense of entitlement that money will always be there, no matter what?

3. How has what you learned from these various sources influenced the way you handle your finances today? For example, are you a spender or saver? Are you savvy about investing? Do you like to spend ostentatiously, or do you love nothing more than a bargain? Is there anything you would like to learn to do better or differently—for example, not spend every cent you earn, or be more generous with your money?

4. What does money mean to you? For example, it could be a source of fun or security, or it could be an anxiety-producing necessity, etc.

5. Do you have any fears regarding money? If so, what are they? For example, you might fear losing what you have, or fear that you'll never have enough.

6. Excluding a mortgage, how much debt are you comfortable with?

7. What, to you, is a "major purchase"?

8. How much household income do you need to feel secure now? In five years? Ten years? Twenty?

9. How do you feel about wives earning more than their husbands? Do you anticipate this as a possibility in your marriage? If so, how comfortable are you with it?

10. Have you and your future spouse discussed how the two of you will handle your finances (checking accounts, credit cards, etc.) post–wedding day? What have you decided? Are you pooling all of your money, or keeping finances separate and dividing joint living expenses?

11. Is there any one thing you dread talking about when it comes to money? What is it and why does it bother you? Is there some aspect of money that you sense your future spouse doesn't like to talk about? What is it?

12. What, if anything, bothers you most about how your future spouse currently handles money? Why does it bother you?

13. Would you like to have children? If so, how many? What time frame do you have in mind for starting a family?

14. Do you expect that one of you will stay at home to care for your children, and if so, who? Have you considered the feasibility of living on one income?

15. Have you ever thought about starting your own business? If so, what would it be? How would you fund it?

16. Do you dream of someday changing careers? If so, what might the new career be? Would it involve going back to school? How would you pay for it?

17. Imagine that you've won or inherited one million dollars, tax free. What would you do with it?

18. Retirement may be a long ways off, but dream for a minute. What would your retirement be like? Where would you live, in what kind of house? What work, if any, would you be doing?

If you and your FH both answer these questions honestly and compare your answers, you should come away with at least a few rich areas of discussion. You may find aspects of your money dreams or attitudes that are quite different to those of your FH. Remember that differences aren't to be feared or avoided—it's highly unlikely that your attitudes and experiences would line up on every topic. What's important is that you're able to respect each other's differences so that you don't get caught up in futile arguments or attempts to change each other.

Naturally, none of the responses or conclusions that you arrive at after answering these questions are ironclad. Complex as we humans are, attitudes, feelings and opinions about money can and do change over time. Who knows how each of you will feel after you've been married for a few years. You may not be thinking of a career change now, but in five years you might feel differently. "You need to leave wiggle room for epiphanies in marriage," notes Joseph Romano, a certified financial planner in Chicago. "This isn't formulaic." Still, it's important to take a look at the bigger picture to make sure your overall goals and dreams and lifestyles are compatible. The more you're able to talk honestly about money now—how to get it, how to spend it—the stronger your marriage will be to handle the inevitable ups and downs that come from managing finances together.

Lisa and Rick are one couple that had the courage to talk openly and face down potential money conflicts before they wed in November 2002. Lisa, thirty-three, is in charge of media relations for an art gallery in Manhattan. Her husband, Rick, also thirty-three, is a film editor. As Lisa explains it, she and Rick are fortunate to come from families with money, but Rick even more so than her. The two first met and dated in college. After graduation they parted ways, only to meet again ten years later and fall in love. Lisa says her first impression of Rick in college was that he was spoiled. "He had a lot of nice clothes, stereo equipment. When he had a crush on me he'd buy me presents. He wasn't the starving student!" Lisa says that when they were dating the second time around she learned that Rick had had a history of problems dealing with credit card debt dating back to his days in college, but that his father always bailed him out. "He'd also lived with a girlfriend for five years, and when she lost her job Rick was supporting both of them. He incurred thousands of dollars of debt." She says the debt, which totaled about $15,000, came from expenditures such as restaurant meals, trips, taking classes and charging them. "I told him I'm not marrying that debt," says Lisa. She asked him to come clean with his father for one last bail-out, which he did.

Even with his financial slate clean, it took time for Rick to get his impulsive spending under control. Before they married, Rick and Lisa had started a side business selling antiques and other merchandise at flea markets and on eBay. Shortly before their wedding, Rick had heard that a Nobody Beats the Wiz! store was going out of business. Without consulting Lisa, he went out and bought $8,000 worth of computer equipment to resell on eBay, putting it on a credit card. "He called me at work, very excited. He said he thought we could make a lot of money. But if computer equipment is six months old, you won't get top dollar." Rick's first thought after getting himself in over his head again was to call his father to help him pay off the credit card debt, but Lisa, trying to help him end a pattern of dependency, stopped him. "I told him, 'We're not asking your dad for the money.'" She says eventually they sold everything, but it was at a loss. "It took over a year to pay off the card," she says.

Lisa says her willingness to confront negative money habits and the couple's ability to be open with each other has made it possible for them to work things out. "If I say that behavior frightens me, or puts us in jeopardy, he makes an effort to stop. I have certain behaviors he doesn't like and he says, 'Please try not to do that.' It's a compromise." These days, the couple avoid credit cards, but it takes discussion and cooperation. "He'll say, 'Let's go get a new sofa,'" she says. "I'll say, 'First earn the money, then we'll go get it.' He's hearing and responding."

Lisa and Rick's story demonstrates just how much give-and-take can be involved in the complicated task of managing money with another person. But it also shows how, ideally, we can complement each other for our strengths and weaknesses. What follows are some typical areas of conflict that you may face as a newly married couple.

## Sticky Money Situations: How to Deal

### When Spender Marries Saver

Psychologists say that opposites do attract, and even if a couple doesn't start out with one as the clear-cut spender and the other the saver, they'll eventually evolve into those roles. "The seduction to buy things is everywhere," notes money and psychology expert Olivia Mellan, author of *Money Harmony*. "We're all brainwashed every minute. If someone has a tendency to spend, that'll probably get worse over time unless it's addressed."

Often, overspending revolves around credit card debt. One spouse is very careful, watching every dollar for fear that they're not on track, while the other takes a live-for-today attitude, running up a credit card balance. This goes on for only so long before things come to a head.

Some brides-to-be, aware that their FH is an overspender (as in the case of Rick and Lisa) insist on change before they head down the aisle. Michele, thirty-seven, works in marketing in Raleigh, North

Carolina. She and her fiancé, Richard, thirty-eight, who works for a major IT provider, have lived together for nearly two years. "I have debt that I'm working on—$6,500—but it comes from student loans and medical expenses," Michele says. Her fiancé's finances are a source of concern to her. "Richard has close to $15,000 in credit card debt," she says. "It just comes from out-of-control spending and back taxes that he didn't take care of. Part of the reason we've waited to get married is to make sure we can stick to a budget for a long period of time and not lose control."

The bottom line is that savers married to spenders need to establish boundaries. Perhaps the nonspending spouse will need to hide the cards away for a while, leaving the spender only with a debit card. This would also be the time to review how much discretionary spending is available to each of you on a monthly basis—along with the goals you're working toward. The conversation about overspending shouldn't be about one of you being "right" and the other "wrong." Instead aim for sorting out the problem *together* so that you can move forward as a partnership.

Ideally, overspending won't become a chronic problem, but if it is you'll need to address it whenever spending gets off track. What you can't do is let your spouse (or yourself!) live beyond your means. It puts you in a hole that keeps you from moving forward, saving and accumulating real wealth.

## When You Earn More Than He Does

According to the U.S. Census Bureau, about 15 percent of wives earn at least $5,000 more than their husbands do each year. Your bringing home a fatter paycheck is only a problem, of course, if it bothers you or your DH (Darling Husband). It seems strange that this might be an issue, given the evolution in the relationship between men and women and the movement toward equality (lest we forget, ladies, we're not totally there, since women still only earn, on average, 76 cents to the man's dollar). Still, many men feel they have to be the primary provider for the family. They may feel insecure or inadequate if they earn less, even if their income is a healthy one. Why? "It goes back to values, and how men are raised," notes Larina Kase, Psy.D., MBA, a career coach who is president of Performance and Success coaching in Philadelphia. "He was probably reared in a home with traditional gender roles." If this describes your FH, he'll need to do some exploring on his own to figure out why he holds onto this traditional idea. It will also help for the two of you to talk it through and strategize ways of dealing with the situation. Perhaps simply offering your assurance that your different pay scales aren't a problem for you will be enough. Or there may be other contributions he could make at home that would make him feel like a more equal contributor, such as taking over more of the household chores. For some men, however, there is only one answer. Nicola, twenty-two, and Jason, twenty-three, have been married for five months. The couple live in Sioux Falls, South Dakota, where she is a computer programmer and he is a sales rep. Currently Nicola earns a bit more than Jason. A problem? "It was a little bit of an issue with him at first," Nicola says. "But now he has a goal: to make more money than his wife does!"

It may not even be a man's traditional upbringing or a self-confidence issue that conspires to make him feel less of a man if his earnings lag. He could also be reacting to social norms. "I think people pay lip service to the idea that it doesn't matter who earns more," says Joan Atwood, Ph.D., director of Marriage and Family Therapy programs at Hofstra University in Hempstead, New York. "If she's the professional, ultimately a problem will hit. Marriage is an economic arrangement. Research shows that the more money you make, the more decision-making power you have in the relationship."

Sheesh, where does that leave us women when we earn less? Ideally in a marriage of equals, the partner earning more—whoever it is—will not hold undue sway over the family finances. Indeed, that can only happen if the partner earning less cedes power, which is what some men in this situation do. "They'll make comments like, 'She makes more and I don't have too much of a say in it,'" notes Atwood.

Anna, twenty-nine, is a federal employee in upstate New York, married to Charles, thirty-seven, who is studying full-time for a master's degree in criminal justice. She says that when Charles was working, they would sit down every other Saturday morning after breakfast to write out bills and discuss their finances. But then as he spent time out of the workforce, "He lost touch," she says. "He lost interest in our finances and would say things like, 'It's all your money anyway.'" Anna says he started to show signs of "feeling like a bum" for not earning money while he was in school. Anna says the situation only turned around once she convinced him that it wasn't her money, but their joint income, and that they needed two heads to keep their finances in order. "We went back to him handling the payment of some of the bills and talking through everything," she says. "It took some time, but he now realizes what his contributions are." As Anna intuitively knew, no matter who makes more money, it's vital in a relationship between equals that both partners remain involved in managing the family finances.

## When One "Comes from Money"

Nowhere is open communication more important than when partners come from highly divergent financial backgrounds. For a man marrying a woman with inherited money, the dynamic may be similar to when she earns considerably more, since for him it may call into question his place as a breadwinner and raise self-esteem issues. Wealthy women may also have the expectation—even if only on a purely emotional level—that her husband should support her. If it's the woman who is less affluent, she may feel dependent on her wealthier spouse, again raising the issue of money equalling power in the relationship.

This could cause resentment on her part, if she has no financial autonomy or say in the family finances.

There may be lifestyle issues to contend with as well, notes Greg McGraime, a Certified Financial Planner and vice president at JPMorgan Chase Bank in New York City. "There could be an expectation of the type of house they'll live in, the model of car they'll drive, the vacations they'll take." It may sound like the nonaffluent spouse has just hit the jackpot, but that person may also feel outside their comfort zone, unless there is full agreement on purchasing decisions. McGraime tells the story of a man from rural Pennsylvania who married into a wealthy Staten Island family. The couple ended up moving into a large house he felt uncomfortable buying, not because he couldn't afford it, but because it wasn't what he was used to. "The couple needs a good understanding of their values and how they'll handle their finances together," notes McGraime. In-laws, too, can contribute to the degree of comfort the less-well-off spouse feels, depending on how accepted he or she is in the family. Naturally, it's up to the wealthy partner to make clear to his relatives where his or her loyalties lie.

In the end, the success of such a union hinges on how well you and your partner love and value each other, quite apart from the money. Work on building a healthy attitude toward your wealth. Try to realize that it's wonderful that you have this, no matter who it comes from. Use your wealth as appropriate, but also make your own money and enjoy life together.

## When Parents Help Out Financially

What could be more thrilling than being indebted forever to a set of control-freak parents or in-laws after they fork over a house down payment?! Actually, a parent helping out doesn't have to be all bad, and we'll get to that. But let's not be naïve. When parents offer to help, you first have to ask yourself, Is this a gift or a trap? Not to worry. We've compiled here a list of questions that should help you to decipher: nice or noose? You then take it from there, either graciously accepting the gift, or slowly backing toward the front door, then turning and running for your lives.

First, let's acknowledge at the outset that parents who want to gift their adult children do it because they love them and want to help them get a financial head start in their married lives. This is a wonderful, generous thing to do, and you are lucky if you or your FH have parents who have the means and willingness to help with something that could take months or years to attain on your own, such as a house down payment. Also, with housing costs being what they are in some parts of the country, a parents' financial boost may make the difference in being able to afford a home at all.

Kathleen and Ty of Irvine, California, have been married for a little over two years. They decided to buy a house during their engagement because they feared housing prices would be out of their reach by the time they married. Kathleen's parents agreed to add $10,000 to the $10,000 she and Ty had saved toward a house down payment. "The money didn't give my parents power in our household," she explains. "But I think ultimately they believed that if they showed us how much they believed in our relationship, and in us, then we would reciprocate by asking their advice for any major decisions. They don't expect us to do what they say, but they do appreciate the fact that we value their experience, particularly when it came time for us to sell our first home to buy our second." The couple traded up after their marriage, using equity from the sale of the first house. "The real estate market is so overpriced now that we never could have afforded our home without it," she says. Kathleen adds that her parents have been generous with other gifts, such as a car down payment, but on occasion they have refused their generosity, feeling it was excessive. "I am Asian and culturally it would be disrespectful to refuse my parents' gifts, but I have had to remind my parents that while their generosity is greatly appreciated, we don't want to sacrifice our independence. My parents do respect that."

Not all parents are as understanding. Thus, in order for a financial gift to be as wonderful and enjoyable as it can be, you'll want to make sure it's not coming with strings attached. So let's get out the manual in our handy Nice or Noose Decipher Kit.

Sometimes, parents are pretty upfront about their intentions and you don't really need the kit. The dialogue would go something like this:

MOM AND DAD: Kids, we want to give you $40,000 toward a house down payment. . . .

YOU: Wow, that's great, thanks so much. . . .

MOM AND DAD: . . . . as long as the house is within one mile of ours, and preferably next door.

Actually, you don't need the kit when you're dealing with loving, upfront parents. What you really need the kit for is loving, yet sneaky parents. You're not sure *what* their intentions are in terms of how involved they'll want to be. Will they expect to come over for dinner every Sunday? Will they want to become involved in how you decorate or maintain the house? Will they feel they have a right to know about your finances? What if there are other boundary issues? In one instance, a man's parents kicked in for the down payment, making his and his new wife's home purchase possible. Nice! Except when his wife started coming home from work, only to find her in-laws in their swimming pool. Noose!

Perhaps this couple would have known the parents felt they had a right to the facilities if they'd followed strategy number one: the straightforward approach. This approach is as simple as it sounds. Here's the scenario. Parents offer to help you with a down payment. You (the child of the parent making the offer) say something like, "We would just love to own our own home. That is so wonderful.

Can you tell us what is expected of us in return?" (And one key thing to get in writing is under what circumstances, if any, they would expect to be paid back.) A frank, yet loving discussion could perhaps turn up something about how they view the situation and how it would impact their relationship with you. But let's say the parents, in answer to this, say "Nothing," and they don't even exchange knowing looks or burst into laughter afterwards. Now it's time to do some sleuthing. Here are questions the two of you should ask yourselves:

- Have the parents given money gifts to other siblings? How did that play out?

- How controlling are the parents in general?

- Do they let you live your lives, or do they often attempt to involve themselves?

- How much of a life do they have? Are they busy with work? Are they involved in activities with friends? Do they travel or take courses? Or are you their life?

- How open and loving is the relationship between the adult child and the parents who are making the offer? If boundary problems were to come up, how easy would it be for the child to talk it over with them?

While the Nice or Noose Decipher Kit isn't foolproof a careful consideration of these questions should help uncover whether or not the offer comes with strings attached. It also makes a difference, of course, if it's your parents who are making the offer or his. If his parents are offering, you should ask yourself how separate your husband is from his parents. Is he a mama's boy? If boundary problems develop, will he speak up? Will he defend his parents, or stay loyal to you?

One way to suss this out is by considering his everyday interactions with his parents. Does he call them excessively (assuming they're in good health)? Does he seem overly dependent? One groom continued to have his mail delivered to his parents' house, even after the wedding took place. It gave him an excuse to go there every day. Just a kid with separation problems? Hardly. He was forty years old! But the icing on the wedding cake came when he put the money the couple had received as wedding gifts into an account he shared with his mother. Noose!

Apart from your FH's relationship with his parents, the other thing to consider is how you feel about accepting their financial gift. How comfortable are you with the idea? How close are you to his parents? How might it affect the balance of power in your relationship with your husband? Could it affect how you divvy up time between your relatives and his? You'll need to have a frank discussion with your FH to address any concerns you might have.

When the stars align, these situations can have a very happy ending. Lisa and Rick, the couple with the credit card problems, knew it would be tough for them to afford a home in the pricey New York tri-state area where they live. Thus, when they decided to marry, they were hoping to have a small wedding and that each set of parents would then gift them with money to put toward a house down payment. As it turned out, their parents went for the big wedding *and* the down payment. Each parent contributed $50,000 toward the house fund, enabling them, along with savings that had been bequeathed to Rick years earlier, to qualify for a mortgage on a $360,000 home in Maplewood, New Jersey. "The mortgage is the same as what we were paying in rent, so that's how we figured out what we would be able to afford on a monthly basis," explains Lisa. "We're close with our families and their helping us hasn't been a problem at all. We're very lucky." Nice!

## When There's Job Loss

Losing a job is definitely one of life's big stressors, and it can test a marriage, particularly when money becomes tight. For the one who loses the job, there can be a loss of self-esteem accompanied by feelings of anger, panic and depression. The spouse who still has a job may feel fearful about the future and finances.

Many times we know when a job loss is coming—there are rumblings about restructuring or downsizing. If this is the case for you or your DH, the best thing to do is to immediately review your budget, cut out a lot of the extras (eating out, concerts) and stop trying to aggressively pay off any debts, if you are in that mode. Now would be the time to send in the minimums due and conserve cash, wherever possible. In addition, the one who suspects a possible layoff should revamp their resume and start putting out feelers for a new job. Networking is still one of the best ways to find a new position, so it would be wise to start making phone calls, arranging meetings with contacts, and getting the word out that you're interested in making a change.

If the axe does fall, give yourself a little time to regroup emotionally, if necessary, before actively job-hunting. It's not a good idea to start going on interviews when you feel angry or panicky—these emotions will likely show through, and no one wants to hire someone who seems desperate or upset. You'll likely have unemployment insurance to tide you over for a while—give yourself time to come to terms with the job loss and consider what you would like to do next.

Naturally, it's important for spouses to keep the lines of communication open when one of you is out of work. You'll each need support and reassurance from each other that everything is going to work out, as it surely will. However, consider keeping the mechanics of the job hunt separate from the relationship. Otherwise, the working spouse can turn into a bit of an unwelcome overseer, checking up and asking things like, "Did you call your old boss like I suggested?" Or, "How many resumes did you send out today?" The job seeker can benefit from a support system that can help him or her be accountable for the job-seeking efforts being made, but it would be better to get that kind of support to come from someone other than the spouse. Other likely sources would include a support group—at no or low charge—or a counselor or a career coach.

One newlywed who weathered the ups and downs of job loss is Meryl, an account supervisor with a PR firm, who is married to Josh, an editor and writer. After their marriage in 2000, the recession hit. Josh was laid off from his magazine job, and freelance work was hard to come by. "The thing about Josh is that he's not one to just sit around," says Meryl. "He was always out there beating the bushes. That made it easy for me to be supportive of his efforts." Trouble brewed between the couple, however, when Josh turned down a good-paying job because he didn't like the magazine that made the offer. "Okay, so it wasn't his dream job, but we needed the money to pay the bills," says Meryl. "I didn't like his sense of entitlement." Josh eventually went back to school to become a teacher and now has steady employment. But their situation points up the many emotional landmines that can come up when a spouse is out of work.

Dealing with job loss is definitely challenging, particularly if it takes a few months to land a new job or to decide on another course of action, such as returning to school or starting a business. Seek outside help and support if things seem overwhelming, and you should be able to come through the period intact, perhaps even stronger as a couple.

## Money Fights: Don't Freak, They're Inevitable

Yes, you're deliriously in love and can't imagine one little cross word ever being exchanged between you two after your glorious wedding day. Actually, in the real world, after the fairy tale celebration is over, it's completely normal not to see eye to eye with your beloved on all matters, including money. There will be inevitable differences to be worked out. What's important isn't that you *have* differences, but how you discuss and resolve them.

Olivia Mellan talks about the power struggle every couple inevitably gets into. As time goes on, she says, men and women tend to polarize around their differences, and then attack each other for them. (Sounds like something I saw on the Discovery Channel between two hyenas fighting over a piece of antelope.) It helps to know that oftentimes fighting about money isn't really about money at all. "It is tied up with our deepest emotional needs: for love, power, security, independence, control, self-worth," says Mellan in her book *Money Harmony*. "And since so many of us are unaware of the emotional load that money carries, we fight about it, without understanding what the battles are about or how to settle them."

What makes this even more complicated is that when couples argue about money, they often don't even start on the same page. Your set of facts may not match up with his set of facts—hence, conflict. In analyzing data from the National Longitudinal Surveys (NLS) spanning from the 1960s to the 1990s, research scientist Jay L. Zagorsky found that most couples have very different views about their income and assets. Half of the couples reported household income that differed by more than 10 percent, and net worth that differed by more than 30 percent. Each sex reported higher income for himself or herself and lower income for the spouse. (Possibly because they reported their own income before-tax and their spouse's income with after-tax dollars.) When it came to assets, husbands reported higher values for property such as home, car and investments, while wives provided higher values for debts. "Helping couples understand that most husbands and wives do not share similar views of the family's finances is a first step in reducing conflicts surrounding money issues," says Zagorsky.

How can couples best structure money discussions to cut down on confusion and unnecessary rancor? One good starting point would be to take a joint look at the actual balance sheets (your net worth, current income and debts) at least once a year. It's difficult to make smart money decisions when you're working with two different sets of figures. Next, it goes without saying that you and your spouse should discuss money matters on a regular basis—at least once a month. How can you best approach these conversations? Money psychologist and financial planner Victoria Collins recommends that you and your spouse think of yourselves as co-CFOs of your family business. When you need to talk about money, set aside time and come together as if you're having a business meeting. Above all, stick to the facts and try to keep the emotion (blame, accusations) out of the conversation as much as possible. Here are some guidelines for running your money meetings:

- Every business meeting has a focus. When you need to talk money, figure out what it is you want to accomplish or what decision needs to be made. If you put parameters around the conversation, it's less likely to segue off into unrelated topics, such as how much time he spends playing video games or how often you get a facial.

- Bring as much information to the meeting as possible. If the purpose of the meeting is to figure out how to pay off a higher-than-usual Visa bill or to reassess your car insurance premiums, bring the relevant statements or receipts so that your conversation will be based on facts.

- Don't fall into impulsive blaming during the discussion or make the other person wrong. "If you hadn't insisted on buying your brother those expensive Rangers tickets. . . ."

- Respect each other's input. Every idea may not be a great one, but you should both have the freedom to brainstorm.

- Be a good listener and don't interrupt. Really try to hear and understand what your spouse is saying. If you're trying to make sense of a decision he's already made, try putting yourself in his shoes.

- If one partner has a stronger financial background than the other, it's incumbent upon that person to explain why, for example, a certain course of action needs to be taken. It's also important for the partner who is less finance-savvy to insist upon an explanation. Even if you find money matters boring, resist the urge to put your head in the sand. In an equal partnership, both understand what's happening with the family business and why.

- Don't get defensive when asked a question about the data, such as, "Why did our plane tickets to your parents cost this much?" Give and take is common in meetings. Again, stick to the facts!

---

**YOUR MONEY MANTRA**

---

Talk about and resolve little problems as they occur. Don't bottle up feelings or wait for a situation to get worse—you'll likely blow up when you finally do broach the topic. The more frequently the two of you can honestly and openly communicate about money, the better your relationship and financial situation will be.

# 3. Plan Your Dream Wedding Without Creating a Big, Fat Financial Nightmare

Each year, approximately 2.2 million couples marry in the United States. From the moment you say "Yes" to Mr. Fab, a giant bridal marketing machine silently moves into place, intent on parting you and your brand-new fiancé (and anyone else who wishes to contribute to your wedding) from your money. The bridal industry generates about $70 billion a year in retail sales; it's little wonder everyone wants a piece of the wedding cake!

These days, the average wedding costs $22,360 and the average one-week honeymoon $3,400, according to The Condé Nast Bridal Infobank. Naturally, those figures can go a lot lower—or a lot higher. Weddings do tend to be considerably more expensive in metropolitan areas, where wages are higher and services cost more. And who's shelling out the cash? According to the Association of Bridal Consultants, 53 percent of weddings today are funded by the couple along with both sets of parents; 27 percent are paid for by the couple themselves, and 19 percent of weddings are paid for by the father of the bride. It's not surprising that many couples are contributing to their wedding expenses. No longer the days when a nineteen-year-old married her beau in a celebration paid for exclusively by her parents, today's couples have typically been in the workforce for a few years and have the means to help finance the kind of wedding they want to have. And the age for first marriage keeps creeping up: The average for women is now twenty-six, compared to twenty in 1970.

## YOUR WEDDING PLANNER CHEAT SHEET
## WHAT TO DO FIRST:

1. Discuss the size and type of wedding you want to have.

2. Figure out how much it will realistically cost.

3. Set priorities and limits for spending.

4. Find out if parents or any other relatives wish to contribute.

5. Start saving, but pay any deposits with credit cards, for consumer protection and frequent flier miles.

## Set Your Budget

The first thing to do, then, after unlocking lips from your first "We're engaged!" kiss, is to set a realistic budget for your big day. What is meant by realistic? One word: affordable. A wedding you can pay for without going into debt or using all of your life savings that may have been earmarked for an appreciable asset, like a house down payment. Here are a few initial questions to guide you in setting a budget:

1. What type of wedding do you want to have? How formal or casual do you want it to be? Consider having a wedding that meshes with your current lifestyle. If you and your family are down-home types, a champagne and caviar fête may not be the best fit. Stay true to your values and focus on having a day that truly celebrates your relationship and the beginning of your lives together. Brides who get swept up in staging an event for show often report feeling let down and depressed when it's over.

2. Where will you marry? Where the two of you live now? Your hometown? His? Or do you have a destination wedding in mind?

3. How many guests will you invite? (The average wedding includes 168 guests, according to the Association of Bridal Consultants.) Remember that guests come with a price tag. The more guests, the more money you'll need to spend.

4. What are your spending priorities? For example, would you rather spend money on a band and leave only a small sum for flowers? Vice versa?

Generally speaking, here's the percentage of your total budget that you can expect to spend in each category:

Reception . . . . . . . . . . . . . . . . . . . . . . . . . . . . . .45%

Wedding dress and veil,
   lingerie, shoes,
   hair/make-up, tuxedo . . . . . . . . . . . . . . . . . .10%

Photography . . . . . . . . . . . . . . . . . . . . . . . . . . . .10%

Music . . . . . . . . . . . . . . . . . . . . . . . . . . . . . . . . .10%

Flowers . . . . . . . . . . . . . . . . . . . . . . . . . . . . . . . .8%

Stationery . . . . . . . . . . . . . . . . . . . . . . . . . . . . . .5%

Rings . . . . . . . . . . . . . . . . . . . . . . . . . . . . . . . . . .3%

Cake . . . . . . . . . . . . . . . . . . . . . . . . . . . . . . . . . .3%

Officiant/ceremony . . . . . . . . . . . . . . . . . . . . . .3%

Transportation . . . . . . . . . . . . . . . . . . . . . . . . .2%

Gifts . . . . . . . . . . . . . . . . . . . . . . . . . . . . . . . . . .1%

Obviously, these percentages will be tailored to your budget, based on what's most important to you. One wedding consultant worked with a bride who had $10,000 to spend—and half that amount was dedicated to her gown! Her attire was the most important aspect of the wedding to her, and she planned accordingly.

In order to set a budget that is realistic and workable, you need to know what things actually cost where you are getting married. It's not enough to read about averages or what somebody's wedding cost in some other part of the country. Talk to a few recent brides, call a few vendors, check out the regional boards on wedding websites to see what you might expect to pay for flowers/photographers/caterers for hundred guests, 150 guests, etc. If you're thinking of getting married in Maui, do some research to get an accurate view of what this would entail. If the number is coming in way too high, obviously you'll need to make adjustments. The most likely place to control spending is by limiting the number of guests and people in your wedding party. You may need to stage a smaller wedding to accommodate your budget. The bottom line when establishing your budget: Once you settle on a figure, you should have a very good idea of what you are going to get and for how many people.

# YOUR WEDDING BUDGET WORKSHEET

| | ESTIMATED COST | ACTUAL COST |
|---|---|---|
| **Ceremony** | | |
| Marriage license | $_____ | $_____ |
| Church donation | $_____ | $_____ |
| Officiant fee | $_____ | $_____ |
| Other | $_____ | $_____ |
| **Reception** | | |
| Food | $_____ | $_____ |
| Liquor | $_____ | $_____ |
| Cake | $_____ | $_____ |
| Location fee | $_____ | $_____ |
| Service fee (wait staff, etc.) | $_____ | $_____ |
| Rentals (tables, chairs, etc.) | $_____ | $_____ |
| **Attire** | | |
| Wedding dress | $_____ | $_____ |
| Veil/headpiece/flowers | $_____ | $_____ |
| Shoes | $_____ | $_____ |
| Lingerie | $_____ | $_____ |
| Hair/makeup (including trials) | $_____ | $_____ |
| Jewelry (other than bands) | $_____ | $_____ |
| Tuxedo | $_____ | $_____ |
| Other | $_____ | $_____ |
| **Music** | | |
| Ceremony | $_____ | $_____ |
| Cocktail hour | $_____ | $_____ |
| Reception | $_____ | $_____ |

## Photography
Photographer     $_____       $_____
Videographer     $_____       $_____

## Flowers
Bridal bouquet     $_____       $_____
Attendants' bouquets     $_____       $_____
Boutonnieres     $_____       $_____
Mothers' corsages     $_____       $_____
Ceremony flowers     $_____       $_____
Reception flowers     $_____       $_____

## Stationary
Invitations     $_____       $_____
RSVP cards     $_____       $_____
Thank-You notes     $_____       $_____
Stamps     $_____       $_____
Other     $_____       $_____
(Calligraphy, reception napkins/matches, save the date cards, announcements)

## Rings
Bride's wedding band     $_____       $_____
Groom's wedding band     $_____       $_____

## Transportation
To the ceremony     $_____       $_____
To the reception     $_____       $_____
Guest transportation     $_____       $_____
Other     $_____       $_____

## Gifts
Wedding favors     $_____       $_____
Attendant gifts     $_____       $_____
Gifts for the parents     $_____       $_____
Gifts for each other     $_____       $_____

Alice, twenty-eight, is a writer and substitute teacher. Her fiancé, Maurizio, twenty-six, is a Lexus mobile technician. They live in Los Angeles, where a wedding can cost as much as a house! The couple has set a $10,000 budget for their wedding, and is putting aside money each month to pay for it. "We knew we couldn't afford a really extravagant wedding, but also we realized we wanted something nice and not tacky," says Alice. "At first Maurizio thought, ten grand, are you crazy? Until I started breaking down the cost of things for him. He then realized it's a very reasonable budget for the number of people we're having."

If you don't have the time to make the necessary calls to get a good ballpark figure or are just flummoxed by the whole idea, consider speaking with a wedding consultant. These pros arrange celebrations such as yours every day, and can give you a good sense of what you can expect to pay for the type and size of wedding that you have in mind. What can you expect to pay for an initial three-hour consultation, which is standard? According to Robbi G. W. Ernst III, president of June Wedding, Inc., and author of *Great Wedding Tips from the Experts* (McGraw-Hill), the fee would run from around $175 to $375. Not surprisingly, fees tend to be higher in large cities. To find a reputable consultant, talk to friends or check The Association of Bridal Consultants at www.bridalassn.com or June Weddings, Inc., at www.junewedding.com. (More on wedding planners, below.)

## Who Pays?

You may already know in advance if either set of parents/stepparents/grandparents will be kicking in some cash. If you don't know, you'll each want to talk individually to your parents, if you feel it's appropriate, to see if they wish to contribute. Give them an idea of what you have in mind—the type of wedding and number of guests—based on your initial thoughts and research. If they do wish to contribute, you'll need to find out how much as soon as possible. It's difficult to plan if you're uncertain of the total amount of money available. If a relative graciously offers to pay for something, such as flowers, you'll still need to know a dollar amount so you'll know how much cash you have to work with. Ideally, anyone who wishes to contribute will give you a lump sum so that you can use the money as you see fit. Of course, when people chip in they may expect to have some say in your decisions so be sure to ask about expectations right away. If you and your FH want to retain complete control, you may want to consider paying for the wedding yourselves.

Note: Once you start planning and making decisions, you'll need to put down deposits with the location site, caterer, etc. Whenever possible, use a credit card instead of a check. That way, if there is a problem with the service or if the vendor closes up shop, you may have some recourse for a refund with the credit card company.

## Don't Go Into Debt

It's fine to use a credit card for protection or convenience, but you will want to have the funds available to pay off the balance throughout the course of your engagement. It's easy to get caught up in spending when planning your wedding. Magazines and books showcase gorgeous dresses, cakes and beautifully decorated reception sites. It's difficult to feel restraint in the face of Martha Stewart perfection, which sends a message that things must look a certain way in order for you to have a wonderful and memorable wedding. (And all I can say is, God bless you if you have the patience to shove a piece of 24-gauge wire up the stem of a delicate flower and shape it, along with one hundred other delicate blossoms, into a densely lush bouquet). In a moment of delirium you may actually ask yourself, is it possible to get married without releasing a flock of doves? The opportunities for overspending seem endless. A 2004 survey by *Modern Bride* revealed that brides shell out over $606 million annually on their prewedding beauty needs alone, including trips to the plastic surgeon and dermatologist for treatments ranging from Botox to liposuction. There's nothing wrong with wanting to look your best, but whatever happened to the bride's natural, radiant glow?

Hopefully common sense will rule. As many brides have discovered, it is possible to have a wonderful, dream wedding at any budget level. Out-of-control spending does not necessarily ensure a day of beauty and elegance. (Especially if you're feeling frazzled and worried about how you'll pay for all of it!)

Lisa, thirty-four, is a customer service representative for a utilities company who also runs her own editorial consulting business. She and her husband, John, forty-five, a recovery boiler operator at a pulp and paper mill, have been married for a year and a half. The couple, who live in Lewiston, Idaho, decided to head to Hawaii with their parents for their wedding, to be followed by a reception at home. "We spent a maximum of $5,000 on airfare, photographer, minister and accommodations," she says. On their return, they spent about $4,000 on a party that included rental of a facility, catered food, fresh leis flown in from Hawaii, wine and beer, a live band and favors that Lisa designed and assembled herself. She says that paying for the wedding and reception was a joint effort. "I made all the arrangements and John and I both contributed to the costs." She notes that her parents generously gifted them with some money, "But we didn't feel as if they needed to do that."

Lisa says that they did not go into debt to have their special day. "We're very glad about that," she says. "We had decided we wanted everything to be simple and special, but not break us. We had a great reception and everyone could be together after the fact, which got us off the hook for going to Hawaii and only inviting our parents."

Julie and John, the couple from Milwaukee who we met in the first chapter, said they tried their best not to go into debt for their wedding. Julie figures that the wedding cost about $10,000, including contributions from both sets of parents. "The thought of going into debt for one day didn't appeal to any of us," says Julie. "We went out of our way to pay cash as much as we possibly could." In the end, the couple only charged a few things, such as gifts for the attendants. "I'm glad we handled it that way," says Julie. "What a relief not to have credit card debt hanging over our heads!"

Even when money is plentiful, due diligence in spending is important. Kathleen's parents picked up the tab for her $50,000 wedding to Ty, but she kept a close eye on the bottom line throughout. "We searched through lots of reference material (books, magazines, etc.) before we made purchases or decisions so that we were sure of what we wanted," Kathleen says. "Buyer's remorse can get very expensive."

The cardinal rule, then, is to plan carefully, be realistic and not go into debt. Do you really want to be paying for your party one, two or three years from now? Let's say you put $5,000 of expenses on a credit card charging 12 percent interest. If you paid a $100 minimum amount due each month (2 percent of $5,000) and didn't charge anything else, it would take you 6.3 years to pay off the balance—and you would end up forking over $2,172 in interest!

Still, if you do feel the need to use a card for some purchases, be sure to select one with a low or zero introductory interest rate for the first few months. (Check out www.bankrate.com for cards with competitive rates.) Then, devise a plan to get the card paid off as quickly as possible—ideally no more than one year after the wedding.

Finally, while you may certainly want to use some of your existing savings to help pay for your wedding, it's probably not the best idea to completely deplete the funds. Everyone needs cash on hand in case of an emergency. And think twice about completely raiding any funds you've put aside for something of appreciating value, such as a house. No one-day party is worth delaying for months or years your ability to build up lasting wealth.

## A Word About Wedding Planners

Why consider using a wedding consultant? The most common reasons are if you don't have the time or inclination to handle the bulk of the planning yourself, or if you're having a destination wedding. The idea is to save you time and, at least indirectly, money. Planners save you time because they have already viewed the work of many of the photographers, cake bakers, caterers and florists in your area and can quickly steer you in the right direction, based on your preferred style and budget. But can a planner really save you money? While that's not a focus of the job, it is up to the planner to track spending and to bring your wedding at or under budget. In addition, a planner who works with a hotel or florist on an ongoing basis knows she'll get a better deal since she keeps coming back with repeat business. The planner can also make suggestions on how you might economize in a certain area without sacrificing quality or appearance, should you decide to splurge somewhere else.

Another way in which consultants may be able to help is through upgrades, according to Gerard Monaghan, president of the Association of Bridal Consultants in New Milford, Connecticut. For example, in negotiating a package a planner who works frequently with a particular photographer would be in a better position to ask the photographer to add on a $16\times20"$ print that would normally cost the bride another $150, or to convince the caterer to upgrade an hors d'oeuvres, by say, increasing the size or number of shrimp being served. A planner may also save you money indirectly if he or she takes care of things that you otherwise would need to take a day off of work for (and perhaps use vacation days that you would rather save for the honeymoon).

If you're considering using a planner, be sure to interview at least two or three to discuss services and fees. You'll also want to make sure there is a good personality fit between you. Here are some questions to ask:

1. *What services do you offer, and how are you paid?* Compensation could be on a percentage basis (of your total budget), a flat rate, an hourly fee or some combination thereof, depending on the package. Note: A reputable planner will not accept commissions or referral fees from vendors, since it's like getting paid twice—once by the vendor and once by the bride. Be sure to confirm that the planner doesn't accept such fees.

2. *Can you help me save money?*

3. *Do you have a contract?* There should be an agreement outlining the fee and the number of meetings he or she will have with you, and with you and your vendors. A contract should also cover what happens in case of a postponement or cancellation.

4. *How long have you been in business?* Obviously, the more experience a consultant has, the better.

5. *What kind of training do you have? What professional organizations do you belong to?*

6. *How many weddings do you handle a year?* (Considering there are four weekends per month, it'll give you an idea of how in-demand the planner is.)

7. *Can you give me references?* Ask for references not only from other brides but vendors with whom the planner works.

8. *Do you have someone to back you up if you are unavailable on my wedding day due to a personal emergency?*

## A Word About Wedding Insurance

If you bought a ring for $2,000, you would certainly have it covered on your homeowner's or renter's insurance policy. A wedding usually costs considerably more. Given wedding insurance's relative affordability, you might want to consider protection in case something goes wrong. Here are examples of what wedding insurance would cover:

- A hurricane rips through town on the day of your wedding, forcing a cancellation. A policy would cover the cost of rescheduling the event.

- Your wedding gown is lost in transit when being shipped to your hometown. Insurance would cover the cost of the replacement, up to the amount the gown was insured for.

- The photographer fails to show up on your wedding day. Coverage would make it possible for you to reunite the wedding party for photos.

- The caterer closes up shop and skips town, taking your deposit with him or her. You would be able to recover the amount you've lost.

The one thing wedding insurance doesn't cover is a change of heart by the bride or groom. If you opt for this kind of insurance, you'll want to carefully read the policy and ask questions to be clear about what is covered, and how much you would be compensated for what could go wrong. As an example of costs, at Wedsafe, Inc., coverage of cancellation/postponement on a $15,000 wedding would run $225.

## Cutting Costs on the Must-Haves

Fortunately, there is an enormous amount of advice available on clever ways to cut costs. If you haven't picked it up already, check out *Bridal Bargains* by Denise and Alan Fields (Windsor Peak Press); it is chock-full of proven ways to save money in every category of wedding planning. Another great source of advice is other brides. Check out the boards on popular wedding websites such as www.ultimatewedding.com and www.theknot.com. No one knows better than recent brides just how to stretch a dollar. Generally speaking, here are the most popular ways to trim costs in the top six categories of wedding expenses:

1. *Your dress.* You may begin with the bridal shops (and remember that they do have sales), but don't end there. Brides shop everywhere for their dresses—at sample sales and bridal outlets, at department and discount stores and consignment shops, on eBay. Consider wearing your mother's wedding gown, or renting one. One bride found a white bridesmaid dress that caught her fancy, while another rather petite bride chose a white prom gown from the juniors' department. Shop wherever there are gowns and you may find your perfect match.

2. *Photography.* To contain costs, limit the number of hours the photographer is on hand at the reception. How many pictures do you really need of your relatives doing the Funky Chicken?

3. *Catering.* The time of day is key here. To really cut costs, get married when people aren't expecting a full meal. You might in-

vite people for tea (3–5 P.M.) or cocktails (5–7 P.M.). Also, don't assume a buffet costs less than a sit-down meal. If you are considering serving a meal, you might want to check the price differences between serving lunch (11 A.M.–2 P.M.), brunch (10 A.M.–3 P.M.) and dinner (6 P.M.–9 P.M.).

4. *Flowers.* Use in-season flowers. Try to avoid getting married around holidays such as Christmas, Valentine's Day or Mother's Day—flowers cost more at these times of year due to higher demand. Add foliage to centerpieces to cut back on the number of flowers used. Consider bridesmaid's bouquets of three to five large blooms (peonies in the spring, hydrangeas in the summer) instead of an arrangement with a lot of small elements. Consider skipping church flowers. You won't be there that long, and the church or other wedding site may be beautiful enough unadorned.

5. *Entertainment.* DJs usually cost less than a live band. When it comes to live entertainment, the main factors are the number of hours played (musicians have minimums, so be sure to ask) and the number of musicians in the band or group. If you're contracting with a band, you could contain costs if a musician plays more than one instrument, or does vocals along with playing an instrument.

6. *Cake.* Have a smaller version of your dream cake made up, along with several sheet cakes of the same flavor, which can be cut in the kitchen. If the cake isn't too complicated, see if a family member can pick it up to save on delivery charges. Don't be afraid to check out a custom-made wedding cake from a supermarket—it will look and taste a lot better than that sounds! Several satisfied brides report having ordered their cakes from places like Albertson's or Publix.

When you marry will also have a big impact on how much you pay for everything. The prime (and most expensive) times to marry are:

**Day:** Saturday
**Month:** May/June, September/October, July/August
**Time of day:** 5:30–6:00 P.M.

## Creating a Plan for the Monetary Gifts You Receive

Of course not every bride expects to receive money as a present. Gifting newlyweds with a check is far more common in the Northeast, for example, than it is in the South. But if you live in an area where you and your FH know some cash is probably forthcoming, it would be wise to discuss what you'll do with the funds. It may be tempting to take the extra cash and simply blow it on your honeymoon, but before you do that consider how you might make the most of your windfall.

Most couples get caught in a debate about whether they should spend or save their wedding money. One thing to consider is whether you're carrying outstanding credit card debt, perhaps even debt from the wedding. Let's say you have a $5,000 balance on a credit card that charges 15 percent interest. It wouldn't make much sense to put the money into a savings account earning 1 percent interest or less. If you have any credit card debt at all, it would be smart to put at least some of the money toward it, and then consider saving or splurging with the remainder.

That's what Julie and John, the Milwaukee couple, did. "We decided we would make a couple of larger payments on an existing loan," says Julie. "But the majority of the money we wanted to spend on *us*. We needed new mattresses for our bed and we splurged on a really nice digital camera."

Here's how other couples spent their wedding money:

*"We purchased registry gifts we wanted but didn't receive, and finished paying for the reception."* —Lisa and John

*"The money went into a savings account. We put it toward the down payment for our house, which we purchased two months after we got married."* —Nicola and Jason

*"We're spending most of it on the honeymoon, and whatever remains on moving expenses."* —Alice and Maurizio

*"We received money from Richard's parents that we were going to put into a house down payment, but circumstances dictated that we had to spend the money on a car after we had an accident."* —Michele and Richard

*"We took $200 for fun money on our honeymoon and saved the rest (approximately $1,500) for home improvement projects."* —Estacia and Chad

*"We used some for our honeymoon to Italy and France."* —Kathleen and Ty

# 4. The Knot Is Tied! Three Things to Do

Once you're married, there are a few things you'll want to take care of right away. The most important, immediate task—if you haven't done so prewedding—is for you and your DH to update any financial accounts that require naming a beneficiary and changing the designee to each other. This is not something you want to let slide for any period of time, for obvious reasons. If you've decided to take Mr. Fab's name, you'll also need to set the wheels in motion for letting the world know that you are now Mrs. Fab. In this chapter we'll review who needs to be informed, in what order, and so on. You'll likely spend a few months covering all the bases, but at least you'll know how to prioritize this task. Finally, you won't want to let too much time pass postwedding before reviewing your tax situation. The last welcome anyone would want to married life is a big fat tax bill from Uncle Sam when you file your first joint return.

Should you change your name? Obviously, this is a very personal decision. Still, it is one your DH may have strong feelings about. In addition, family members—yours and his—may feel the need to weigh in on this question, although the only opinions that really matter are yours and your DH's.

The main reasons brides give for changing their name to that of their husband include tradition, because it adds to the feeling of oneness with their DH, and because they want to have the same name as their children. Some key reasons brides give for *not* changing their name is because they've established themselves professionally with their maiden name, because they want to honor their father or because they don't want to lose that part of their identity. Brides seeking the best of both worlds say that they drop their original middle name and now use their maiden name as their middle name, taking their husband's surname as their own. Of course, some brides also go for the hyphen, opting to use their maiden and their DH's last name together. In addition, some brides change their name to their husband's socially and legally, but continue to use their maiden name professionally. Fortunately there are several options, but ultimately the choice is yours!

# 1. Play the Name Change Game

Obviously you'll only need to do this if you decide to change your name in any way, by taking that of your DH or by hyphenating your two surnames. You can't start playing this game until you get a certified copy of your marriage license, which should arrive in the mail from the town clerk's office where you applied for the license about a month after the wedding. The certified copy of your marriage license is very important: It's the only legal proof you have that you are now Mrs. So and So. It's a good idea to order a couple of extra copies when you apply for your license, in case one gets lost. Sure, you can always order another one later, but having a spare saves the time and trouble should you need it.

Your first stop in the name change game will be Social Security—you'll need to apply for a new card with your new name on it (your number will stay the same). This is an important step since it ensures that you get proper credit for future earnings as reported by your employer. It is your earnings, of course, that will determine your future benefits. To take care of this change, all you have to do is show up at your local Social Security office with proof of both your maiden and married names. A copy of the application (Form SS-5) can be downloaded at www.ssa.gov. The Social Security site lists all of the documents that qualify as acceptable forms of identification, but if you have a driver's license or current passport, you'll be covered. While your application can be mailed along with your proof of identification, I'd recommend doing this in person. For one thing, I wouldn't want to put these sensitive documents in the mail (they would also then get mailed back to you by the agency). In addition, you probably need your driver's license on a day-to-day basis and can't have it held up in the Social Security office. If you have any questions that can't be answered on the website, call Social Security at (800) 772-1213.

The **IRS** automatically updates your name, once it passes through the Social Security system, so you needn't worry about informing the IRS. (As if.) It takes about ten days for the IRS to update its system once Social Security processes the change.

Next you'll need to get a new driver's license and, again, it simply involves proving your old and new identity. Check your state's **Department of Motor Vehicles** (DMV) website for information before schlepping to the offices and the DMV's notorious wait lines. You can very likely download the application form, as well as verify exactly which forms of identity you need to bring. You should also update your name on your car's registration; again, your state's DMV website can instruct you on what to bring.

Your financial accounts are another obvious priority. Let your **Human Resources department** at work know about your change of name and marital status. You'll need a new health insurance card; in addition you'll want the name on your paycheck (or direct deposit) to match the name at your **bank,** which is where you are heading next. If you are maintaining your old checking account you'll of course want to change your name on it. Next contact **any other financial institutions** with whom you do business, such as where you have investments and savings. Then there are the places where you owe money, such as your car loan, credit cards and student loans. In some cases, such as with credit cards, you may be able to handle the name change over the phone. In others, you'll need to visit the offices (such as your bank's branch) with the certified copy of your trusty marriage license and your old driver's license (again, doing that "here's the old me/here's the new me" thing).

It's extremely important that you contact all three **credit reporting agencies** listed below to give them your new marital status and married name. You'll want to be sure that the good credit you've built up under your maiden name gets combined with your new, married identity. Remember, too, that a short credit history (if your records are not combined) will have a negative impact on your score. Call each of the agencies to inform them of the change; they will ask you to fax a copy of your marriage license. Then, get a copy of your credit reports a few months later to make sure your reports have been properly updated. Equifax: 800-685-1111; Transunion: 800-916-8800; Experian: 888-397-3742.

Here's a list of other places that will need your new name; you can tackle them as you live your life (i.e., pay bills or go on an appointment):

Mortgage/landlord
Utilities
Phone/cell phone
Car insurance
Doctors
Lawyer
Accountant
Registrar of voters

Subscriptions
Memberships: alumni associations, gym, video store, etc.

You'll also need to update your **passport**. Go to http://www.travel. state.gov/passport_services.html for the application form and address where you should send it, along with your old passport and a certified copy of your marriage license (a photocopy is not acceptable). It takes about six weeks to get your new passport.

## 2. Update Your Beneficiaries

You and your lovely newly minted husband need to change your beneficiaries so that you name each other in the event that anything happens to either of you. Where have you named beneficiaries that need to be updated?

Your 401(k) plan at work
Any life insurance policy offered at work
Any other life insurance policy you've purchased
IRAs
Savings accounts
CDs
Mutual funds

## 3. Consider Adjusting Your Withholding

You will most likely file a joint tax return with your husband (there's more on taxes in chapter 11). Your joined salaries could bump you up into a higher tax bracket, which means you could owe more in taxes. But you don't want to get stuck with a big tax bill on April 15 (nor do you want to end up with a refund, which is tantamount to giving the government a tax-free loan throughout the year). In order to come out even, how can you figure out how many exemptions you each should now take?

You can use the worksheet that comes with the W-4 form that you get from your Human Resources department. The IRS site (www.irs.gov) has a calculator: http://www.irs.gov/individuals/article/0,,id=96196,00.html, but using it may be a lengthy process as it involves figuring out your taxes for the following year. You could also try the withholding calculator under "Tips & Resources" at www.turbotax.com, which is pretty straightforward. But here's a fairly simple way to do the calculation, courtesy of Eva Rosenberg, MBA, EA (www.taxmama.com):

1. Each of you should locate last year's tax return. Look for the line that reads "Total Tax Liability" on each of your returns. Add the two together. That's the minimum tax you need to pay to avoid a penalty. The rule is, you have to pay 100 percent or, if you received sizeable salary or other taxable income increases during the year, 110 percent of last year's tax liability to avoid an underpayment penalty.

2. Get your most recent pay stubs. Look up the line on each person's stub that shows how much federal tax has been withheld year-to-date. Add these two numbers together (the amount withheld to-date from his paycheck with the amount withheld so far from yours). Note: If you had any previous jobs during the year, add in that federal withholding, too.

3. Subtract the total amount you've both paid in so far (the figure in Step #2) from your combined Total Tax Liability (the figure in Step #1). That's how much more you have to collectively pay this year. Now it's just a question of figuring out how much

comes out of each of your paychecks so that you hit that amount.

4. Look at the pay stub of whoever makes less. If that person doesn't change their withholding, how much more will be deducted from their paycheck through the end of the year? (To figure that out, look at the amount of federal tax that is withheld for each pay period, and multiply that by the number of pay periods left, a figure you can verify with your HR person.) Subtract that amount from the figure in Step #3.

5. The new number in Step #4 indicates how much the higher-earning spouse needs to have deducted by the end of the year. The rest should be simple. Take this figure and divide it by the number of pay periods left for the higher-earning spouse. That's how much needs to be deducted from his or her remaining paychecks. Ask the HR Department to figure out how many exemptions you would need to claim to equal that number, and adjust the withholding accordingly.

## AN EXAMPLE

STEP 1: Let's say your total combined tax liability is $20,000.

STEP 2: Let's say the amount of federal tax withheld from your paychecks so far this year totals $7,000.

STEP 3: Subtract $7,000 from $20,000. Together you still need to pay in $13,000 by the end of the year.

STEP 4: Figure out how much more the lesser-paid spouse will pay in federal taxes if he/she makes no adjustment to his/her withholding. To do this, go back again and look at the amount of federal tax withheld from each paycheck of the lesser-paid spouse. Multiply that figure by the number of pay periods left. Let's say you have $158 taken out of every paycheck for federal taxes, and there are nineteen pay periods left in the year. $158 \times 19 = \$3,002$. (Let's round down and use $3,000.) Subtract $3,000 from $13,000, the figure in Step #3. You still need to pay $10,000 by the end of the year.

STEP 5: Let's say there are nineteen pay periods left for the higher-paid spouse, who is going to make up the difference. $10,000 divided by 19 is $527. The higher-earning spouse needs to make sure that is the amount of federal tax withheld from the next nineteen paychecks.

After planning your wedding, you may feel you never want to see another "To Do" list again. But if you take care of these three important must do's, you could save yourself from potential headaches later.

# 5. Managing Your Money

Chances are, you've been managing your money for at least a few years on your own. The difference now, of course, is that for the first time you'll be doing it with your best friend and lover. The purpose of this chapter is to guide you through setting up basic financial house-keeping with your DH. Initially we'll discuss just how joined you want your finances to be and review the options available for merging accounts. You will also have an opportunity to create a new budget, based on your joint income, and determine how you will divvy any expenses that need to be divided between you. Most important, there is an exercise for you and your DH to discuss your money goals. You've undoubtedly had discussions about how you would like to spend your money and what you would like to work toward as a team, but now you'll have a chance to commit these goals to paper, prioritize and set a timeline for reaching those that are most impor-tant to you. We'll also review the best ways for staying on track to meet your goals—beginning with paying yourself first. Finally, our housekeeping wouldn't be complete if we didn't review how you'll collectively tackle bill paying, organizing and maintaining financial records.

Managing money postmarriage is no big deal for some brides; for others there are worries about a loss of autonomy and independence. Whichever camp you fall into, this chapter can help you sort through the issues and set up accounts with your DH in a way that is most comfortable for the two of you. Remember that whatever decisions you make, they are always subject to review and revision. Some brides need time to fully join their finances with their DH, and that's okay. Like life, managing money is a continuum. Whatever form it takes, the idea is to keep moving forward and making smart choices for building wealth. This chapter can help you set the foundation for doing just that.

## Your Bank Accounts: To Merge, or Not

This is one of the biggest decisions newlyweds initially face after tying the knot, although some couples take steps and combine accounts even before they've made their union legal. Should you merge your accounts? Should you keep them separate? Should you do a combination of both?

How do others do it? In a *Smart Money/Redbook* 2003 money and marriage survey of 1,016 married or cohabiting adults, 64 percent of the men and women who responded said they maintain joint bank accounts; 18 percent had a combination of joint and separate accounts, and 14 percent kept everything separate.

Of course there is no one right or wrong way of managing your money. Some people feel they need to combine accounts right away as a sign of their commitment. Others ease into it, keeping separate accounts while opening up a joint one. Those who want to maintain a strong sense of autonomy maintain individual accounts. It's really a matter of personal taste, depending on your personalities. Some people worry that if they don't combine accounts something is wrong with their relationship. But not combining accounts only means what you make it mean. If you're both comfortable with keeping everything separate, are open and upfront with each other about your finances, and are working toward mutual goals, so be it. For those couples who are still on the fence, let's take a closer look at the options.

## Meet the Mergers

Some couples choose to pool their resources completely, with all debts paid out of joint funds. Diane, twenty-six, a child-care provider in Chelmsford, Ontario, Canada, and her husband of nearly two years, Richard, twenty-five, a computer networking consultant, combined their money and their lives one month after they met! "Once we moved in together, we opened an account and both of our incomes went into it. We would just pay the bills from that account," says Diane. The couple is currently working to pay off student loans and credit card debt so that they can eventually save for a house. "To us it's not his money or my money, it's our money," Diane adds. "I really don't understand the concept of his money, my money. It's going to the same place—to pay bills and for extra money for a night out, so why make things more complicated than they have to be?"

Michelle, thirty-seven, who works in marketing, and Richard, thirty-eight, a payroll manager in Raleigh, North Carolina, have also closed out their individual accounts in favor of joint checking and savings accounts. Together they're paying down debt—her student loans and medical bills, and his credit card debt. As Michelle puts it, "While I understand why some couples keep their finances separate, I believe that maintaining joint finances really tests the level of your commitment, which can be hard, but rewarding, when you meet goals together. If you're coming together as life partners, it seems that ultimately you have to partner financially." She says that in one respect it's easier to have joint accounts because the spending limits are more clearly defined. "I have someone to 'rein me in' when I'm thinking of indulging myself, and vice versa," she says. However, they have built some fun into their spending plan. "We've budgeted times throughout the year when we can treat ourselves to something extra like a weekend out of town, or a pro football game."

Danielle, the New York City writer and Oren, the accountant, come from opposite ends of the spectrum when it comes to handling money—she never had to worry about it growing up; he did. Given their backgrounds, the couple struggled mightily to sort out how they would manage money after marriage. Says Danielle, "My parents taught me to know the value of money, but they also conveyed the message that money would always be there. For example, my dad would tell me I had to get a summer job during college to teach me a work ethic. But then once I earned the money, he'd say put that away and he would pay my bills." Oren's family history was nearly the opposite. The youngest of six siblings, his mother died when he was thirteen and his father when he was eighteen. After his father passed away he was taken care of by his older siblings, particularly an older sister who became like a mother figure. "Oren learned to save and hoard," says Danielle. "I, on the other hand, never had to think twice before buying anything."

The couple lived together for a year before they married. "It's good that we had that year to iron out any issues," says Danielle. "Before we got married I had all these plans in my head about how to share finances. I was terrified of him being too strict with how I spent my money. On the one hand I was learning how not to spend money I no longer had, since my father wasn't paying my bills anymore. At the same time Oren had to understand he couldn't make me feel bad if there was something I wanted to buy, because I was working also. We had to compromise a lot." The couple worked hard through trial and error to reach a comfort zone with each other. "He had to learn to trust me, that I wouldn't spend a lot of money frivolously. I had to learn to trust him that he wouldn't yell at me for what I did spend."

These days, the couple have two checking accounts and a joint savings account, all of which are linked. Danielle explains that Oren pays the rent and the American Express bill, and she pays the utilities. They are saving aggressively for a house down payment and are also looking forward to starting a family. "It took us a long time to figure out how to talk to each other," Danielle says. "We fought a lot, but in the end we learned how to communicate with each other."

My DH and I also fall into the "joint accounts" camp, but we ended up that way by default. It was a second marriage for both of us and we'd been handling money on our own for several years. We didn't discuss combining accounts after marriage—we just held on to our individual checking accounts and decided who would pay which bills. He paid the mortgage out of his account and I paid the rest of the bills with mine. A few years later we both got downsized from our jobs and started consulting/freelancing from home. When our direct deposit paychecks went away, it no longer made sense to have two accounts—plus it was easier to meet the minimum for free checking with just one. Our arrangement primarily works (at least from my point of view) because my husband has no interest in micromanaging our money. Naturally, he looks at our statements when they come in the mail, but the minutiae of daily spending is of little interest to him, which is a good thing. (If he knew what I spend on highlights, he'd *plotz*.)

## Merge the Money Scorecard

### PROS

Simplifies bookkeeping
Both can feel control of pooled money

Strong sense of working as a team

Easy to coordinate savings and investments

## CONS

Every purchase open to potential scrutiny

One person might zone out of money management and let spouse make all the decisions

Puts assets at risk if one partner is in a business prone to lawsuits (i.e., a physician)

## Keep It Separate

Kathleen and Ty, the California couple whose parents helped them with their first house down payment, are working toward saving for a baby and retirement. For them, keeping individual checking, savings and investment accounts makes all the sense in the world. "Ty and I both have money automatically deducted from our paychecks for retirement savings, so what's left over is for the bills, and what's left over after that is what we call our discretionary funds to spend as we wish," Kathleen says. "If we are planning a large purchase, then we adjust the automatic deduction from our paychecks for whatever we are saving for." She notes that they've received a bit of grief from their friends for having separate accounts, but it doesn't bother them. "Doing it this way gives us a chance to really discuss our finances and keep each other informed," Kathleen explains. "So many couples we know don't discuss their finances because they see the joint checking account statement and most of the time the only thing they discuss are the items that make them angry, like purchases at the mall or the happy hour bill. Ty and I feel we are adult enough to pay the bills and keep track of our own spending and saving. We each enjoy the financial independence. People, by nature, tend to get territorial and once you've commingled funds, it seems like every single expense has to be some grand production where both parties need to agree or veto it." For this couple, separate accounts allows them to manage their money effectively with fewer headaches.

If you and your DH decide to keep things separate, don't be surprised if you get some flak from family or friends (which might be one good reason not to discuss your banking habits!). It can be threatening to some, who may unjustly question your level of commitment to each other. Some couples want to keep things separate simply because they're used to handling their money on their own and don't want to lose that sense of independence, even though they are still working toward joint goals. Others have such divergent investing styles that keeping accounts apart is the only way they can sleep at night. The fact is, not everyone feels the urge to merge—if this way works for you and your DH, that's all that counts.

## Keep It Separate Scorecard

### PROS

Each maintains a strong sense of autonomy and independence

Fewer fights over personal purchases

Protects assets if one spouse is in business prone to lawsuits

Makes it easy to keep premarital assets separate (no commingling of funds)

### CONS

Couples may not coordinate savings and investments, making it more difficult to reach joint goals

Potential for couples to keep each other in the dark about their finances

Spouses don't have easy access to each other's funds—a potential problem in case of emergency. Each spouse should have a TOD (transfer on death) put on their checking accounts, naming each other. It's also vital for spouses with separate accounts to have power of attorney or springing power of attorney documents signed, in case one spouse dies or becomes unable to handle his/her affairs.

With this document in place, spouses can access money in each other's accounts and make decisions about how it is spent or invested. Otherwise, you would have to hire an attorney to petition the court to become the incapacitated spouse's guardian or otherwise access the funds. While doable, this would be a costly and time-consuming step to have to take during an already difficult time.

## Yours, Mine, Ours

Julie and John from Milwaukee have a hybrid arrangement that includes individual checking accounts along with a joint checking and savings account. "We each deposit our half of the monthly expenses into the joint checking account and the rest of the money is ours to do with as we choose," says Julie. "That way, each of us is still handling our money in a way that's comfortable for us." They pay for their own credit cards, and Julie makes a student loan and car payment out of her account. Their joint savings account is earmarked for a house down payment—their goal is to accumulate $10,000 within the next two years. "Neither of us is a huge spender, but we each have our thing that we like to splurge on. I frown a bit when he spends a lot on his hobby (slot car racing/diecast car collection) and he frowns a bit when I spend a lot on groceries. I like to cook and experiment with recipes. But we work it out. He uses his personal spending money for his hobby. Groceries come out of our joint money and on weeks that

I've spent a lot, the next week I'll go more bare bones and spend less."

Heather and Jason, the Orlando couple, hashed out the specifics of their "his, hers, ours" accounts premarriage. The couple, who moved in together during their engagement, opened a joint checking account to which they each contribute 56 percent of their incomes for paying bills and joint purchases. Heather says that after marriage they plan to open a joint savings account—their house fund—to which they will each deposit 10 percent of their salaries. The remaining 34 percent will go to individual savings accounts for purchasing personal items, such as video games, manicures and gifts for each other.

Nicola and Jason have a total of six bank accounts between them! Explains Nicola: "We have a joint savings and checking account. The checking account is for paying our bills and our savings account is money set aside for vacations. In addition to those two accounts, we each have our own savings and checking accounts. We are on each other's accounts but we manage our money and spend it how we please. If the other is running a little short that month we help each other out." Right now the only debt the couple have is their mortgage, which they're working to pay off in twenty-five instead of the traditional thirty years.

There's a strong case to be made for the hybrid arrangement, particularly in the early stages of marriage. It's hard to know exactly how you and your spouse will handle money until you've actually started doing it together. Opening a joint account while maintaining individual ones is a good way to see how the two of you will operate as a financial team. You can always merge everything later if you choose. Some experts believe it's important for women, especially, to maintain an individual account throughout marriage. "Women especially have a need for autonomy," says money psychologist Olivia Mellan. "Of course you're going to work toward goals together. But the joint account shouldn't be all the money you have." She also thinks separate accounts are important for the reason Kathleen espouses—simply so you don't have to account for every penny you spend and "sneak purchases in from the mall." But it works the same for men, too. "Let's say each has a hobby the other thinks is silly," says Mellan. "I don't think they should argue about the expense every time one of them goes out to buy something."

## Yours, Mine, Ours Scorecard

### PROS

Function as a team while maintaining some autonomy

Fewer arguments over personal purchases

Gives spouses a chance to see how they each manage money before merging

### CONS

Bookkeeping is more complicated: several accounts to maintain

Potential for disagreement over how much each contributes to joint account

Couples may not coordinate savings and investments, making it more difficult to reach joint goals

Puts assets at risk if one partner is in a business prone to lawsuits

## Still on the Fence?

Are the two of you still undecided about what to do? Or does one want to merge while the other wants to remain separate? Trite as it sounds, sometimes time can assist in working things out. Consider that one in-depth, longitudinal study found that prewedding, more men than women said they wanted to keep their finances separate, but that tends to disappear after marriage. Social psychologist Margaret S. Clark in the department of psychology at Carnegie Mellon University in Pittsburgh has been tracking 108 couples for the past eight years. The couples were first interviewed six weeks prior to marriage. Her findings showed that before marriage, a full 57 percent of the participants said finances should be merged, although more men than women thought things should be kept separate, usually because they earned the higher income. Six months after the wedding, 54 percent thought finances should be merged, but there was no difference between the responses of men and women—the men were just as comfortable with the idea of joint accounts.

Clark further found that if someone truly doesn't want to pool resources, it's because that person tends to be less trusting of people in general, not specific to his or her partner. "This trait—the lack of trust—does show up prior to the marriage," notes Clark. So presumably, there shouldn't be any surprises. In addition, Clark found that those who don't want to merge finances also tend to keep track of everything else, such as who took out the garbage or did the dishes last. "People who have trouble trusting others don't think their needs will be met," says Clark. If this situation could play a part in your marriage, it would be wise for the less trusting mate to seek counsel to see how he or she might learn to feel more secure.

## Setting Money Goals

Now that you're focused on getting your married finances in order, you'll want to be clear about the financial goals the two of you will be working toward. You undoubtedly have a few things in mind, as does your DH. If you haven't done so already, now is the perfect time to put all those ideas on the table to discuss which you'll target first.

Writing down goals is a proven way of increasing our chances of meeting them. When we put thought to paper, it becomes more concrete—and attainable. The following exercise gives you and your DH a chance to discuss and determine specific financial targets, along with a realistic time frame for reaching them.

While this is certainly a time to let your mind go and think of all the possibilities, there are a few "must" money goals you'll want on your list, along with the plasma TV. These would include "paying down debt if you have it, buying a house if you rent, creating a savings cushion equal to six months of after-tax income, and starting to put some money away for retirement," notes Andrew G. Altfest, an investment advisor with L. J. Altfest & Co., Inc., in New York City. He notes that making a decision that would enable a spouse to increase future earning power, such as saving for a master's degree, is another worthwhile goal during a couple's early years of marriage.

Several brides interviewed for this book felt that retirement was too far off to worry about now. If you fall into this category, this notion hopefully will be banished by the time you finish this book! As you work on your list, seriously consider including retirement savings in your long-term goals, if you haven't done so already. Estacia, twenty-seven, a law student and professional fund-raiser in Indianapolis, and Chad, twenty-eight, a business manager who is also studying for a law degree, are one couple that did list retirement as one of their top three goals, along with paying off student loans and saving money to remodel their 1920s English Tudor–style home. While Estacia doesn't feel they're saving enough, "We're doing what we can without zapping all the fun out of life!" she says. Still, the couple has only been married for four months, so there's plenty of time for improvement. Now it's your turn to decide what takes priority.

## Exercise: Write Down Your Goals

You should each work separately at first. Use the form below or a separate sheet of paper to state what you would like to achieve with your finances. Make each goal specific, and put a price tag next to it—an estimation will do if you don't know the exact cost. Include a deadline next to each goal, and place them in order of importance.

Short-term goals, if any (6 months or less)
1.

2.

3.

Medium-term goals (1 to 3 years)
1.

2.

3.

Long-term goals (3+ years)
1.

2.

3.

Now it's time to compare lists. Don't be surprised if there are some differences between you, particularly where time frames or priorities are concerned. One of you may want to buy a new car while the other wants furniture for the house. He may want to focus on the house down payment but you think the credit cards should be paid off first.

How can you resolve your differing points of view to come up with a cohesive, going-forward plan?

It's important that each of you have a chance to fully express your desires and perspectives. In having this discussion, be careful not to make the other person wrong. "Yeah, like we need a powerboat," you might harrumph. Try to understand each other's point of view, and to ferret out the emotional "need" that the "want" might be satisfying. Is it about financial security? Is it about owning something as a reward for hard work? Whatever it is, try not to discount it or pass judgment on it. We only tend to feel angry and resentful when we sense that we're not being taken seriously by our spouse.

As you go through your lists, look for similarities. Where are areas of agreement? You'll likely need to come up with a compromise or two as you finalize your list. The idea is for the conversation to end on a win-win note, with each person getting something of what's most important to them.

John Gottman, Ph.D., is a professor of psychology at the University of Washington and a relationships guru who has studied how hundreds of couples interact and argue about all manner of topics, including money. As he states in his book, *The Seven Principles for Making Marriage Work* (Three Rivers Press), one of the goals of marriage is to help each of you realize your dreams, and the extent to which you each can do that plays a big factor in how happy each of you are in your marriage. "Whatever your disagreement over finances, you'll defuse the tension by working as a team to devise a plan you both can accept, even if it doesn't give you everything you want right now," he says. He further recommends that couples revisit their goals every so often—say, once a year—to make sure they're still in agreement and/or on target.

## Tips for Reaching Your Goals

Once you've hashed out your lists and prioritized your goals, **write down the top three.** For example: House down payment: $30,000 by 6/30/06. **Post your goals in a prominent place** where you will see them each day—perhaps the refrigerator door or inside the doors of your bedroom closets. The list will remind you, each time you glance at it, of why you're making the sacrifices you're making—such as not going on monthly weekend getaways—to reach your targets.

You'll also need a **plan for monthly savings.** Divide the cost of the savings goal by the number of months you have to reach it, and you'll know how much to put aside for each one. Admittedly, this figure will be an ideal. It's tough to save aggressively for multiple money goals. You may want to put the bulk of your savings into your top priority goal, just to reach one faster.

Next, **open one or more money market or savings accounts** for each goal. (Make sure you're not paying high maintenance fees if you go under a certain balance. If that's the case, you might have to use one account for more than one goal.) **Set up an automatic deduction from your checking account** into the funds. Don't leave monthly savings to chance—have the money transferred before you even see it. Be sure to make your goals, along with corresponding monthly payments, a line item when writing your budget (which is coming up in the next section).

If you find that you're having trouble meeting your savings targets, try keeping track of your spending for a couple of months. Do you see areas where you might be frittering money away, or overspending? Be honest: Did you really need that $200 Prada wallet? (Note to self: Uh, maybe?)

Let's face it. It can be difficult to maintain discipline around spending, especially when opportunities abound to part with our cash. If you miss a deadline for reaching a goal, don't worry. Just keep working at it. This is the only way to build wealth. A bonus here, a raise there—you can accelerate and make up for lost time. The point is that you have something you're working toward. Without targets, you and Mr. Fab could easily spend everything you earn and what would you have to show for it? If you're like me, you'd have a designer wallet with a now-broken zipper. Don't go there, sister.

## Creating a New Budget

You and your DH undoubtedly each had a budget when you were single—even if the numbers were sort of loosely jingling around in your heads. Now that you're a twosome, it's time to come up with something more concrete that will take into account your combined incomes, expenditures and the money goals you just hammered out.

Before you begin, however, it's important for the two of you to know exactly how your discretionary income is currently spent. Thus, you and your DH first need to do a little exercise over the next month or so called Track Your Spending. Why? Because, without tracking your spending, how do you really know how much you're doling out each month on going to the movies/paying the dry cleaner/eating out/and yes, drinking those blasted lattes at Starbucks? All you need to do is get a couple of small notebooks. Then, each of you should write down everything you spend your money on over the next four weeks, along with the amount.

Once you've tracked spending, categorize your purchases (clothing, entertainment, eating out, etc.) so they can be added to the budget. You're now ready to come up with a basic money plan. In a big picture way, you want to devise a plan that allows you, with the income available, to:

- Cover your monthly expenses

- Live within your means

- Avoid bad debt (credit cards)

- Be adequately insured

- Maintain an emergency fund

- Fund retirement accounts

- Save for your money goal(s)

It sounds like a tall order, but with careful planning and some discipline, you should be able to create a budget that moves you toward your goals while taking care of the basics. The effort will be well worth it as you watch your accounts grow!

# BUDGET WORKSHEET

*Include **monthly** figures.*

## WHAT'S COMING IN

### Income (net, or after taxes)

Her: . . . . . . . . . . . . . . . . . . . . . . . . . . . . . . . $_____

Him: . . . . . . . . . . . . . . . . . . . . . . . . . . . . . . $_____

Other Income: . . . . . . . . . . . . . . . . . . . . . . . $_____

**TOTAL:** . . . . . . . . . . . . . . . . . . . . . . . . . . . . . $_____

## PAY YOURSELF FIRST

Emergency Fund: . . . . . . . . . . . . . . . . . . . . . $_____

401 (K) Her: . . . . . . . . . . . . . . . . . . . . . . . . . $_____

401 (K) Him: . . . . . . . . . . . . . . . . . . . . . . . . . $_____

IRA (Her): . . . . . . . . . . . . . . . . . . . . . . . . . . . $_____

IRA (Him): . . . . . . . . . . . . . . . . . . . . . . . . . . . $_____

Savings Goal #1 _____: . . . . . . . . . . $_____

Savings Goal #2 _____: . . . . . . . . . . $_____

## WHAT'S GOING OUT

*(List your combined expenses)*

Mortgage/Rent: . . . . . . . . . . . . . . . . . . . . . . . $_____

Electricity/Gas: . . . . . . . . . . . . . . . . . . . . . . . $_____

Water/Sewer/Trash: . . . . . . . . . . . . . . . . . . . . $_____

Telephone: . . . . . . . . . . . . . . . . . . . . . . . . . . $_____

Cell phones: . . . . . . . . . . . . . . . . . . . . . . . . . . $_____

Cable/Internet: . . . . . . . . . . . . . . . . . . . . . . . $_____

Groceries: . . . . . . . . . . . . . . . . . . . . . . . . . . . $_____

Lunches out: . . . . . . . . . . . . . . . . . . . . . . . . . $_____

Meals out (all other): . . . . . . . . . . . . . . . . . . $_____

Car payments: . . . . . . . . . . . . . . . . . . . . . . . . $_____

Car insurance: . . . . . . . . . . . . . . . . . . . . . . . . $_____

Gas: . . . . . . . . . . . . . . . . . . . . . . . . . . . . . . . . $_____

Parking/Tolls: . . . . . . . . . . . . . . . . . . . . . . . . . $_____

Public transportation: . . . . . . . . . . . . . . . . . . $_____

Credit cards (all): . . . . . . . . . . . . . . . . . . . . . $_____

Charge card (e.g., American Express): . . . . . . . . $_____

Drugstore/Prescriptions: . . . . . . . . . . . . . . . $_____

Therapy: . . . . . . . . . . . . . . . . . . . . . . . . . . . . . $_____

Health/Dental insurance: . . . . . . . . . . . . . . . $_____

Life insurance: . . . . . . . . . . . . . . . . . . . . . . . . $_____

Student loans/Tuition: . . . . . . . . . . . . . . . . . . $_____

Laundry/Dry cleaning: . . . . . . . . . . . . . . . . . . $_____

Clothing: . . . . . . . . . . . . . . . . . . . . . . . . . . . . . $_____

Gym memberships: . . . . . . . . . . . . . . . . . . . . . $_____

Entertainment: . . . . . . . . . . . . . . . . . . . . . . . . $_____

Newspapers/Magazines: . . . . . . . . . . . . . . . . $_____

Housecleaning: . . . . . . . . . . . . . . . . . . . . . . . . $_____

Charitable donations: . . . . . . . . . . . . . . . . . . . $_____

Haircuts: . . . . . . . . . . . . . . . . . . . . . . . . . . . . . $_____

Pets: . . . . . . . . . . . . . . . . . . . . . . . . . . . . . . . . . $_____

Mad money (Her): . . . . . . . . . . . . . . . . . . . . . . $_____

Mad money (Him): . . . . . . . . . . . . . . . . . . . . . . $_____

Other _____: . . . . . . . . . . . . . . . $_____

Other _____: . . . . . . . . . . . . . . . $_____

Other _____: . . . . . . . . . . . . . . . $_____

## A Word About the Emergency Fund

It's so easy to just skip putting money into this account. Doesn't it always seem like there are so many other things to buy or do with the money that would otherwise go into the fund? There's a sale at Nordstrom's (who can resist?) or you want to take a romantic weekend trip (you've been working so hard!). There's nothing wrong with those things. But before you do anything, make sure you are consistently putting money into your emergency fund.

The purpose of the emergency fund is to have cash on hand to see you through financial emergencies that cost more than your regular budget allows for. Your car needs a new transmission; the hot water heater bursts. You lose your job and it takes you longer than anticipated to find a new one. You don't have dental insurance and you need a root canal. Your reserve fund ideally will get you through these circumstances—or at least hold you in good stead until your situation improves. Without money to fall back on, you could find yourself falling further and further behind, and perhaps borrowing money in ways that could damage your finances for a long time to come.

In the past many people, myself included, thought they could use their credit cards as backup in case of an emergency. If you're running a little short, you might reason that you'll just put the car repair or dental bill on the card, or use it to cover living expenses during a bout of unemployment. This actually used to work okay. Unless you had bad credit, you could usually get a card with an excellent interest rate and pay the card off over time. But these days, given the way some credit card companies treat their customers, using credit cards as a backup is a dubious proposition at best. There are card companies that think nothing of raising your interest rate to 20 or even 25 percent, even if you have no history of late payments and pay more than the minimum due. (Card companies call it "repricing" when they suddenly increase a customer's interest rate. I like to think of it as a legal form of "loan sharking.") Perhaps they have decided they don't like the fact that you're near your credit limit—even though it's a credit limit they themselves approved and offered to you! You are suddenly a "credit risk." If you have a balance that you are unable to pay off right away and your interest rate suddenly hits the ceiling, you are in deep trouble. That's because with every payment you make, you are paying an enormous amount of interest that makes the bank a lot richer and you a lot poorer. Let's say, as an example, that you have a credit card with a balance of $7,800 at an interest rate of 7.9 percent. The finance charge would be about $50 a month. A waste of money to be sure, but things could be a lot worse. Now let's say the card company decides to raise your interest rate to *24.98 percent.* You would need to pay the bank $171 *in interest alone* before you've paid any principal.

The best thing that consumers can do to protect themselves from this type of scenario is to maintain a reserve fund for financial emergencies. Think of it as "credit card insurance." In the event of an emergency, you'll pay out of your cash fund without falling into credit card spending, which will ultimately cost you more.

That said, you should aim for saving at least three to six months of salary to cover most emergencies. Some would say that if you're in an industry offering little job security, or an industry in which it's hard to find a new job, you should actually have a year's worth of salary set aside. Obviously it would be much more challenging to reach that goal, but shoot for three months to start.

Nicola, the computer programmer from South Dakota and her husband, Jason, already have five-and-a-half months' worth of salary set aside in an emergency fund. Saving comes naturally to Nicola. "That's what my parents taught me," she says. "That it's always fun to have money on those rainy days." She points out that the only debt they have is their house—and that's how they plan to keep it.

Where should you stash your emergency cash? Naturally you'll want to keep the money liquid so that you have ready access to it. You might keep it in a savings or money market account at your bank. The interest you earn will be negligible, but the money is there and the balance you maintain may help you meet the minimum for free checking. Once you start to build up your emergency fund, you could use some of the money to buy one or more Certificates of Deposit (CDs) from a bank or savings institution and earn a little higher rate of interest. CDs are bought for three, six or nine months or more (the longer the term, the higher the interest rate) and thus could be bought on a staggered basis. If you do have an emergency, you're not likely to need all the cash you've saved at the outset. You could keep the first three months' of savings completely liquid and the second three months' worth in staggered CDs. If you're going to buy CDs it's important to ladder the maturity dates, because if you had to cash out early, you'd have to pay a penalty or give up some of the interest you earned.

## A Word About Paying Yourself First

Many young couples today live paycheck to paycheck. They have too much debt or simply spend everything they earn and can't seem to get ahead. If this describes your situation, this section is especially for you. The way to stop that paycheck-to-paycheck cycle and to start building wealth and financial security is to pay yourself first. Unless you do it—or at least give it a try—you'll never have any money left over to put toward your goals, your retirement or your emergency fund.

The way to pay yourself first is to **let it happen automatically** so that you never even see or miss the money from your checking account. Have $50 or $100 automatically deposited into your "emergency fund" savings account once a month. Set up an automatic deposit into your IRAs, if that is how you're saving for retirement. Don't leave it to chance; it's too important to your future financial well-being. This is the only way to build wealth—you need to **spend less than you earn** and invest the money where it can grow over time. Once you see the balance in your statements begin to increase, chances are you'll be encouraged to find new ways to cut costs and sock even more toward your savings goals.

## Three Tricks for Staying Within Your Spending Plan

Let's say you each have your designated amount of mad money for the month, but sometimes you're tempted to go beyond. Certified Financial Planner Victoria Collins has these ideas for what to do when you're dying to buy something that maybe you shouldn't:

1. Tell yourself to wait 48 hours, then reevaluate the purchase. If it's still that important, buy it.

2. Figure out how many hours you would have to work to pay for the item. Is it worth two or three days' of salary? Or even a half day's worth of work?

3. When you're feeling like a spineless jellyfish in the face of temptation, don't instantly make the purchase. Stop, pull your little notebook out of your purse and write down five other things of equal value that you could buy. Do you still want it?

The idea is to take some of the emotion and impulsiveness out of shopping. Once you look at potential purchases from a numbers perspective, the item may not have as much appeal as it did before. The idea isn't to stop buying everything, but to buy on more of a rational, needs-based basis, rather than an emotional one.

## How Will Expenses Be Divided?

You've got your budget written, now it's time to put it into action. By now you should have figured out how you are managing your bank accounts—joint, separate or a hybrid of the two. If you and your honey prescribe to the one-pot theory of finance, you very likely have both of your paychecks deposited into one account and pay all of the bills from there, so there is no need to divide expenses. Divvying up household expenses need only come into play if you're handling your money separately, or doing the combo of joint and separate.

If you're keeping things separate to any degree, the first thing you need to figure out is which bills you're paying individually (e.g., your own credit cards and student loans) and which you're paying together (e.g., the rent and utilities). Of the ones you're paying together, you then need to calculate how much each contributes, based on income. If you and your DH make about the same amount of money, you can simply split the shared expenses in half.

But sometimes one spouse makes considerably more than the other, and that's where trouble can brew. It isn't just a question of splitting everything; each contribution should be representative of how much you add to the household income. For example, if he is earning $100,000 to your $50,000, it would only be fair if he puts in 66 percent of the expenses to your 34 percent. Otherwise he'll be flush a lot of the time while you'll be broke.

Estacia and Chad, the two law students, are one couple who have figured out an equitable division of expenses, based on income. In addition to maintaining separate checking accounts, they opened an interest-bearing joint account to which they each contribute for the monthly mortgage payment and savings. "Chad puts in a little more than I do since he makes more," says Estacia. "He also pays most of the household expenses, such as gas, electric, phone, cable and his boat payment. We each make our own car and insurance payments as well as our own credit cards and student loans. I buy the groceries and pay for other extras, like eating out, cell phones and family gifts."

## Bill-Paying and Organizing

The important point here isn't so much who writes the checks or makes the electronic bill payments, but that you are both knowledge-able about your finances, the budget and the goals you're working to-ward, and that you both remain so. Sometimes when one partner takes over the bill-paying, the other sort of fades out of the financial picture. The uninvolved partner can lose track of the budget and what the limits are and start overspending. Or the spouse who pays the bills ends up making all of the decisions. Down the road the unin-volved partner wakes up, starts looking at the finances and questions how things were handled.

This is a scenario you want to avoid—and it's one that's more com-mon than you may think. Doug Charney, a certified portfolio man-ager and president of The Charney Investment Group in Harrisburg, Pennsylvania, says that countless times, newlyweds have come into his office for consultation and more often than not, the wife has built up more savings than the husband. What happens? The men take over handling her investments—and the women let them. This is ob-viously a big mistake. "Both spouses need to be involved in the decision-making," he says. "The couple should work as a team." Charney further points out that women tend to do a better job of in-vestigating investments and other financial matters, and are able to work more effectively with money pros. Men sometimes have an "I know better" attitude—even if they don't!

Some couples decide to trade off on the bill-paying/money manage-ment responsibility—for one couple, that meant taking turns every other year. This is a great strategy—but oftentimes the trade-off never occurs.

One way to keep both of you in the loop is to have the one who isn't actually paying the bills to file the paperwork, or to scan the bill into your computer if you keep electronic copies. In addition, consider establishing a set time at least once a month to go over bills and the month's spending. These meetings provide a chance to go over any unusual expenses that may be coming up, such as needing new tires for the car, and to review your savings.

Many couples figure out fairly quickly who is taking the lead when it comes to getting the bills paid on time. Alice, twenty-eight, the writer and teacher, and Maurizio, twenty-six, the Lexus mobile technician from Los Angeles, said there was no question that she would be in charge. "We've merged our accounts and since I am the more fiscally responsible one, I will be handling the family budget. We're working on paying down our bills first—I have student loans and he has credit card debt—and then we'll be saving for a house or future vacations. We both knew we'd be better off if I took the reins on this one."

Kelly, twenty-five, an administrative services assistant, explains that Matt, twenty-six, an engineer and her husband of nearly two years, pays the bills out of their joint checking account. "He just wanted to have the control more than I did," she says. Since Kelly was managing her father's estate when the bill-paying decision was made, she didn't push back. "I was a little hesitant to let him handle the entire checkbook because I was used to doing that myself—and even for my parents," she says. "As young as ten years old, I was writing checks for my grandmother because her handwriting was too shaky. But Matt has done a good job of maintaining it."

Things don't always go so smoothly, particularly when there is no system in place. Lisa, the PR director for a Manhattan art gallery, says her and her husband Rick's lack of organization around bill-paying has caused some conflict between them. They each have their own checking account and a joint savings account at the same bank, all of which are linked, along with individual savings and investments that are kept separate. "We pay our own bills and we take turns paying the mortgage, depending on who is more flush that month," Lisa explains. "I'm not that great at the organization that goes into paying bills. But suddenly I'm not the only one responsible so I can be a little scattered, and Rick picks up the ball." Still, without a system, things can get confusing. "In a way it's like roommates," says Lisa. "Every bill is not paid by the same account. Or by the same person! One thing that's a challenge is where do we put the bills. Sometimes I'll find a bill and it doesn't look like it's been paid." This is where trouble can start. "We don't have a tone with each other except when it comes to money," Lisa says. " 'Well, did you pay that bill? It doesn't say so.' We've been working at ironing out a lot of this stuff."

These days, overlooking a bill and paying it late—especially a credit card bill—is serious business. It could mean getting hit with a dramatic increase in your interest rate along with a late fee as high as $35. Thus, when it comes to household bills, consider putting one person in charge while keeping the other updated on the state of your union. Here are other bill-paying anxiety-busters:

- Keep all unpaid bills in one place. I keep our bills in a straw basket in an otherwise empty file drawer. They're out of sight (which is nice—who wants to constantly look at a stack of bills? Yuck!) but I know exactly where they are.

- Consider paying bills as they arrive in the mail. This is especially easy to do if you pay online. With a few clicks you can pick a date for having the debit made from your account, and you'll never have to worry about "Did I or didn't I?"

- Consider using Quicken or Microsoft Money software for paying bills and keeping track of your spending and saving. It's an easy for way for you and your DH to know exactly where things stand.

## Maintaining Good Financial Records

What could be more boring than making sure your financial records and other important papers are neatly filed in the appropriate places? The good news is that once you get a system in place and get things filed, it's not something you need to repeat—you just need to maintain your files. And what a joy it will be to know you can locate the details of your health plan within one minute! I have a metal file cabinet for this stuff. But if you have no need for an entire file cabinet, you can get a cardboard file box for the same purpose.

What follows are general guidelines for what to keep and for how long. If you want to err on the side of safety, keep important papers like tax returns or those pertaining to a house sale for several years after the fact, just in case. Here's what you'll need to file at home:

**Bank statements and canceled checks.** Keep these for a year with two exceptions: Keep canceled checks for home improvements indefinitely. You'll need those for when you sell the house—any monies used to improve the property could reduce the size of your capital gains. Other canceled checks for tax-deductible purchases should be weeded out and put in your working Tax File.

**Bills (credit cards, utilities, etc.).** Keep for one year, for budgeting purposes. (You can total and divide by twelve to see what you're really spending each month on gas, electricity, etc.)

**Brokerage account.** Keep annual statements, dividend reinvestment statements and confirmations of all trades each year. Your accountant will need this to figure out taxes you owe on any gains. As discussed previously, hold onto statements indefinitely that are sent before or at the time of marriage.

**Car insurance policy.** The insurer will send a new copy each year when you renew. This is the only copy you need.

**Car loan.** Keep the loan agreement in your file at home. The title, if you have it, will go in your safe deposit box.

**Car repairs.** Keep receipts for all maintenance and repair work. You may need these documents if your car is under warranty to prove your upkeep of the car.

**Employment records.** Letters of recommendation, etc., should be stored in one file for easy reference.

**Home purchase.** Hold onto all documents that you get at closing.

**Homeowner's/renter's insurance policy.** In addition to keeping this in a file at home, put a copy in your safe deposit box. If disaster strikes, you'll have quick access to it.

**Household inventory.** If there were a fire in your house, would you remember all of your possessions? Not likely. That's why it's important to start an inventory list, perhaps keeping it in an Excel spreadsheet for easy updating. For clothing, count how many you have of everything—shoes, pants, coats, etc. Then go from room to room and make note of each possession you have, along with the brand or model number. Keep receipts of all expensive items and put them in your safe deposit box, along with a copy of your household inventory. If you can't bear the thought of compiling a list, at least walk through your house or apartment with a camera or camcorder and take pictures of all the rooms and your possessions. Don't forget your closets. Keep this visual record in your safe deposit box.

**Insurance.** Maintain separate files for your health, disability and life insurance policies. A copy of your life insurance policies also goes in your safe deposit box.

**IRAs.** Keep the statements and annual report. Be sure to hang onto the statement that indicates the balance in your account at the time of marriage.

**Mutual fund statements.** Keep your year-end statement. Also keep statements that indicate the balance at the time of your marriage.

**Pension plan.** Keep all documents your employer sends you related to the plan, including statements and plan descriptions.

**Property tax.** The payments are tax deductible, so keep the statement in your working Tax File.

**Student loans.** Hold onto your original agreement and monthly statements.

**Tax file.** Keep a file where you can throw any receipts throughout the year for purchases that may be tax deductible. When it's time to prepare your taxes, everything will be in one spot.

**Tax returns.** Keep for at least three years from the date the return is due, along with all supporting receipts. However, if you filed for an extension, the three-year minimum starts when you actually filed your taxes.

**Warranties.** File these away until they expire.

**Wills.** Neither of you have one? Hopefully by the time you get to

the end of this book you will! Once you have your wills written, you'll keep the original at your attorney's office, plus a
copy in your files and safe deposit box.

## What Goes in a Safe Deposit Box?

It's not that it would be impossible to get a duplicate of most of these
records, but it would be time-consuming and not necessarily hassle-
free. Keep these documents (along with small valuables) at the bank,
for safekeeping:

Birth certificates

Car titles/car lease agreements

Coin/stamp collection

Divorce decree

Homeowner's/renter's insurance policy (copy)

Household inventory lists
and photos/video of
possessions

Important contracts

Jewelry

Life insurance policies

Loan documents

Marriage certificate

Military service papers

Mortgage deed

Receipts of major purchases
and home improvements

Savings bonds

Stock certificates

Record-keeping is one of life's more onerous tasks, but think of
how freeing it will be once it's done. Your payoff comes on the day
you need a copy of that insurance policy—and you know just where
to find it.

# 6. Managing Credit and Debt

Credit Cards: Which to Cancel, Which to Keep

Once you marry, you'll want to review your outstanding credit cards and decide which accounts to keep open and which to close. You'll also want to answer the all-important question of whether the two of you will open a joint account together.

Typically many of us walk around with a wallet full of credit cards. According to Cardweb.com, Inc., every American with at least one credit card has 2.7 bank credit cards, 3.8 retail credit cards (store, gasoline) and 1.1 debit cards. How many do you and your DH have between you, and how many should you have? As always, there's no "right" answer, but there's little to be gained from keeping open accounts that are rarely used. Here's a strategy for sorting through the plastic:

- Go through your wallets and consider which cards it would be advantageous to keep. Obviously you'll want to hold onto a card with an attractive feature, such as a low interest rate or frequent flier miles. If you have a short credit history, think twice before closing your oldest card; it'll ding your credit.

- Consolidate your debt onto the one or two cards that you decide to keep. But you need to be careful in how this is handled. Credit card companies today look for any excuse to raise your interest rate, and one of those excuses is if you are close to your credit limits. If, then, you will be using more than 35 percent of your available credit as a result of transferring the balance, don't do it. Call the card company first and see if they will raise your credit limit (explain that you want to consolidate debt onto their card). If the answer is yes, get the credit increase and then make the transfer.

- Don't add each other's names to the card or two that you each keep. It's important for each of you to have your own credit. You don't want to ever find yourself unable to open a credit card on your own, without the benefit of your joint income. "My husband and I have kept our own separate cards," says Julie, the secretary from Milwaukee. "I've heard horror stories of women who only had joint accounts with their husbands. Then they had a hard time if their husbands died or left them because they had no credit rating on their own." Which is exactly why you should keep at least one card in your name only.

- If you do decide to close out an account, do it properly. Call the creditor to let the company know you're closing the account. Ask the customer service rep to indicate on your credit report that the file was closed by the consumer, and ask for written confirmation. Send a follow-up letter to the creditor. The next time you check your credit report, make sure not only that the account was closed, but that it was recorded properly as closed by you.

## Should You Get a Joint Credit Card?

If you both have great credit histories, there's no reason not to open a joint account if you want one. But if one of you has blemishes on your report, you'll need to think carefully before applying for credit together. For starters, you won't qualify for the best rates. Second, if one of you has trouble handling credit, it puts the other partner at risk. If you get credit together and there are late payments or non-payments or things otherwise go wrong, the partner with the good credit will see it go south. Generally speaking, don't combine credit if one of you has:

- A bankruptcy that is still reported on the credit report.

- A history of late payments or defaults.

- A judgement or tax lien assessed.

- A history of being an overspender. Don't get a joint account until it's clear the account won't be abused.

In fact, many financial experts believe there is no reason why couples should feel the need to rush into getting a joint credit card. No matter how well you may think you know your spouse, you learn a lot more once you're actually living together and can observe his money habits firsthand. Many experts counsel caution and allowing the marital relationship to develop before jumping into joint credit cards.

## Good Debt Vs. Bad Debt

If you're like most couples, you've come into your union with debt—most likely student loans, credit cards, maybe a car payment, even a mortgage. Some of this is good debt—like a house, which is an appreciating asset, or an education loan, since it can lead to a better-paying job. The rest is "bad debt," meaning you end up with nothing of real lasting value. You and your DH will probably not be able to avoid bad debt 100 percent of the time throughout your marriage. But it's a worthy goal to work toward—for example, to save for a car and pay cash instead of taking an installment loan, or to save up for that vacation instead of putting it on a card. The worthiest goal of all is to not carry a balance on credit cards. Remember at all times that balances on credit cards represent loans. When you consider buying something that you can't pay off right away, be it a new stereo or a new coat, ask yourself, is it really worth borrowing money for this?

Many of us have not been living within our means for quite some time. Learning to live with the cash we have (actually, spending *less* than we have, so that there is money left to save and invest) requires an adjustment in thinking. It requires going against the full power and force of every advertiser and marketer in this country whose intent is to get us to part with our money. Don't you absolutely have to have the new cell phone with the latest gadget? (Everyone dances around so cute in the commercial!) Or the new iPod with the longer battery life? Or the designer jeans that cost well over $100? As a country we don't put a lot of stock in saving up for the things we want or need. How 1950s! Although, in fairness, back then people also weren't bombarded with easy credit offers as we are now. Many of us would like to at least appear wealthier than we are, so we buy things we can't really afford, putting them on credit cards. We want to get that Saks Fifth Avenue look even though we have a Target budget. But as many couples mired in debt have learned (some of them as a result of the wedding!) they may have the (temporarily fashionable) goods or the latest electronic equipment, but they don't have wealth or peace of mind as they struggle to pay the bills each month. Perhaps we could start a new trend, one that encourages less stockpiling of debt and more accumulation of savings. We may not end up with the most expensive pair of pants on the block, but we'd have awfully attractive bank statements!

## How to Get Your Cards Paid Off

No one knows better than I do the weight you can feel from carrying around credit card debt. I was a single mother for several years and used a couple of cards to tide me over when funds were short. I used the cards for clothes for my son and myself, and also for things that weren't part of my regular budget, like trips home for the holidays, Christmas spending and the like. The problem is that I never got around to paying off the balance, and ended up with some serious credit card debt. Finally resolving to pay off the debt was a difficult, but very important challenge. If you have made paying off credit card balances one of your money goals, here's a strategy for getting the job done:

1. Make a list of all of your credit card bills, their interest rates and the minimum monthly payments due. Figure out how much of your discretionary income you are able to put toward your debt reduction goal each month.

2. Target one card to pay off first. This could either be the card with the highest interest rate, or it could be a card that you would be able to pay off fairly quickly, giving you a psychological boost.

3. Pay as much as you can on the one card, and continue to pay the minimum amount due on the others. Don't forget that charging anything new on any of these cards will defeat the purpose of this exercise!

4. Once you've got your first targeted card paid off, add the amount you've been paying on the first card to the minimum due on the second card you're about to tackle. Example: Let's say on the first card you were paying $375 per month—$75 as the minimum amount due, plus an additional $300. Once you're ready to tackle card #2, add $375 to the minimum due on that card.

5. Want to figure out exactly how long it will take you to pay off each card, taking into account not only your monthly payment but the interest you pay each month? Check out the budget calculators at www.choosetosave.org.

6. Keep telling yourself "cash is king!" You'll end up paying a lot less for the things you buy when you stop paying interest on top of the purchase price.

Until your cards are paid off . . .

• Make sure you're paying the lowest interest rate possible. Call your existing cards and ask if they will lower yours. Mention another, better card offer you have on hand and see if they will meet it. Note that you can only do this if you have been a good customer, paid your bills on time, and have good credit. If you are not a stellar bill-paying citizen of the world, two words: Don't bother.

• Some cards today offer zero percent interest for up to twelve months. Consider rolling your balance over to one of these cards, but be sure to find out what the APR would be after the introductory period is over. Obviously you want it to be as low as possible if you continue to carry a balance. In any case it shouldn't be more than 14 percent. In a recent Consumer Action survey of 140 cards by forty-five issuers, the average interest rate was 11.9 percent, so see how much better you can do than that. If you roll over a balance, make sure you don't have to pay a transfer fee, which could range from $10 to $50. Some companies waive the fee for new cardholders if they immediately transfer the balance when applying for the card, so be sure to ask. To find a new card deal with competitive terms, check out www.bankrate.com, www.cardweb.com or www.cardratings.org.

## When Shouldn't You Pay Off Your Cards?

This section will read like blasphemy. We've been talking about paying off debt, living within our means, spending less than we earn and saving the rest, etc. But are there times when you *shouldn't* make paying off credit card debt a priority? If your card or cards are at a high interest rate and you're unable to get the balances shifted to a lower-interest card, you should pay them off ASAP. But aside from that there are other considerations: Namely, how did you and/or your spouse end up with high credit card debt to begin with? Were the cards used for clothes, vacations, "stuff" you couldn't really afford? Or was the credit used for medical expenses, or during a period of unemployment when it was needed to make ends meet? Sometimes, when dealing with our money, we have to realistically consider how much self-discipline we have. If you pay off the credit cards knowing you won't run the balances up to the limits again, getting rid of the balances would be the prudent thing to do. But if you know you're going to be back up at the limit in a year or two, you're better off paying them down over time at a low interest rate. Then, use the extra cash you would have used to pay down the cards for a different money goal, like a house down payment, and put some aside for an emergency fund. The sooner you can develop the discipline not to rely on the cards for extras, the better. But in the short-term, focus on other money goals if it's clear you're not ready to stop whipping out the plastic.

## Whose Debt Is It, Anyway?

Debt you bring into your marriage is still your debt, unless you decide to put each other's names on the account—then it becomes joint debt. Generally speaking, combining premarital debt is not a good idea. Let's say you each come into the marriage with student loans and decide to consolidate them to get a lower rate. Should the marriage break up, you would be equally responsible for the entire amount. Suppose, then, he defaults on the portion he's supposed to pay for one or more months. It would not only hurt your credit rating along with his, but the lender could come after you to collect the missing payments.

What about debt incurred during marriage? According to Robert J. Nachshin, a founding partner in Nachshin & Weston in Los Angeles, debt incurred during marriage is community property. You both own it, except if the debt is totally unrelated to one of the spouses. What does that mean? It includes specific types of debt exclusive to one spouse, such as gambling debts or expenses related to infidelity (e.g., plane tickets to Tahiti charged to a credit card). In divorce cases, soon-to-be exes either decide how they're going to divvy up their debt or a judge does it for them. Problems can arise, however, when debts are in both of your names. A judge may order him to pay off your jointly held Visa. If he doesn't, your credit gets dinged along with his, and Visa would come after you for the payments as well.

With the exception of community property states, debt incurred in your name only during the marriage is yours and debt incurred in his name only is his. You would only be responsible for a spouse's credit card debt if you were a coapplicant on the card (or loan) and signed the application, making it a joint account. A spouse listed as an authorized user of the card is not responsible for the debt.

The one time you would be liable for debt in his name only (and vice versa) is if you live in a community property state and the debt is accrued during the marriage. Let's say your spouse opened up a few credit cards and ran up the balances. If you were to split, you would also be responsible for the debt. Community property states include Arizona, California, Idaho, Louisiana, Nevada, New Mexico, Texas, Washington and Wisconsin, and the territory of Puerto Rico.

## Debt Consolidation: When and Why?

You've probably heard about consumer credit counseling or debt management programs that are able to negotiate with creditors to bring down high interest rates, stop late fees and work out repayment programs for consumers with out-of-control debts. These groups can help you to get your finances on track, but only if you are in over your head and unable to make minimum monthly payments. It's not a strategy for lowering interest rates and getting debt paid off more quickly—it's a tool for people in financial distress.

If you have legitimate need of a consumer credit counseling service, you need to be careful in selecting a company to work with. Once you understand how they operate, you'll see why. The debt counselor reviews your budget with you to figure out how much you can pay your creditors each month, then he or she develops an acceptable repayment schedule with your creditors. You send your payment directly to the credit counseling service each month, who pays off your creditors. Should you have need of a debt consolidation program, you can find a reputable one through the Association of Independent Credit Counsel-

## GOT BAD CREDIT?

If your credit report is in a state of disrepair, you will want to make fixing it a priority, but avoid credit repair clinics at all costs. They cannot do anything to "fix" your credit that you can't do yourself despite their claims to the contrary. If you have bad credit, you'll need to systematically work to repair it, which will take some time. There's no quick fix to a history of late payments or a bankruptcy, which stays on your record for ten years. To begin to improve your credit report, make payments on existing loans on time and don't go over your credit limits. Pay more than the minimum if possible. If you're starting over, open a secured credit card, perhaps from the bank where you have your checking account. With a secured card, you deposit a specified amount of money in an account, you're issued a bank credit card and the amount you've deposited becomes your credit limit. Using this card, make small purchases and pay off the balance each month. You could also start a positive history of repayment with a gasoline credit card or department store card (if you know you won't go overboard charging), or by taking out a small personal loan from your bank.

ing Services (www.aiccca.org) or the National Foundation for Credit Counseling (www.nfcc.org). Ultimately you'll want to work with a debt counselor at a nonprofit agency that is certified by one of these organizations. When you call, verify that the person you are speaking with is a certified debt counselor, not a telemarketer who is trying to sign you up for a debt consolidation program, regardless of your needs. While it's certainly possible to work with a debt counselor long-distance, there is something to be said for being able to visit the company offices and see exactly where your money is going.

It is common for credit counseling agencies to charge a start-up fee and monthly charge, so be sure to find out how much that is, and get it in writing. A hallmark of a nonprofit is that the fees should be quite reasonable. According to the NFCC, in 2002 the average cost of a budget counseling session was $13, the average Debt Management Plan enrollment fee was $23, and the average fee for monthly services was $14. Also be sure to clarify that when you make your first payment, it is going to your creditors, not toward the origination fee. If the company keeps your first payment to cover costs, you could end up being late with your creditors.

## Student Loan Payoff Strategies

Many newlyweds come into marriage with at least one partner saddled with education debt. In fact, the average amount of debt students carry at college graduation is $20,000, with about $3,000 attributed to credit cards, according to Robert Manning, professor at the Rochester Institute of Technology and author of *Credit Card Nation.* The good news is that the student loan debt is probably at a fairly low interest rate, compared to other types of credit, and the monthly payments are manageable. But debt is debt, and while it may not bury you, it's still a draw against other financial needs and goals.

If you have not yet consolidated your student loans, that should be your first line of attack, since you can most likely reduce your interest rate. In 2004 interest rates on Stafford loans, the most common type of federal student loans, hit a thirty-nine-year low of 3.37 percent for those in repayment. The first thing to look into is consolidating your government-backed loans through your lender. Once bundled together, the interest rate becomes fixed and you don't need to worry about future increases. The fixed rate is based on the weighted average of the interest rates on the loans at the time you consolidate, rounded up to the nearest one-eighth of a percent. In any case, the interest rate won't exceed 8.25 percent. Even if you only have one loan, you can consolidate, so don't hesitate to make the call. Note: If your loan balance is $7,500 or less, you can only consolidate through your current lender.

Even after consolidating to a lower interest rate, lenders may be willing to further sweeten the pot. Many will reduce your interest rate by an additional .25 percent if you sign up for automatic bill payments at the time of consolidation. But the incentives don't end there. Some lenders will drop the interest rate an additional full percentage point if you make on-time payments for a set period of time, usually three or four years. Some offer rebates. In 2004, College Loan Corporation was offering a 1 percent cash rebate of the balance on your loan after only six months of on-time payments. Let's say you had a $30,000 consolidation loan locked in at 2.6 percent to be repaid over 20 years. After six months of on-time payments your balance would be $29,425.80, and you'd get a 1 percent rebate check for $294.25— the equivalent of almost two months of payments. Most lenders do offer incentives, so if you're thinking of consolidating it's important to shop around.

If all of your loans are through one lender, that company has the first right of consolidating your loans. (Although in 2005 Congress may vote to drop this requirement via the Reauthorization of the Higher Education Act, the legislation that sets the rules for federally backed student loans.) If, however, you request an income-sensitive repayment schedule from your lender (that means your payments are adjusted each year based on your gross monthly income) and you are refused, you have the right to check out the offerings of other lenders to see if they'll give you that type of repayment plan. If you're like most borrowers, however, you received your federal loans from more than one lender, so chances are you'll be able to look around for the best deal. It's important to consider your options carefully, since you're only allowed to consolidate once, unless you take out another student loan.

If you have Perkins loans, consider leaving them out of the consolidation package. There are circumstances in which up to 100 percent of the Perkins loan can be forgiven. For example, teachers in schools that serve students from low-income families, special ed teachers and teachers specializing in subjects where there is a shortage, nurses or medical technicians, law enforcement officers, Vista or Peace Corp volunteers and those who serve in the military could qualify to have some or all of their loans forgiven. However, you lose that benefit if you consolidate, so if you think you might qualify, leave the Perkins loan out of the equation.

Finally, think carefully about extending your payments over a longer period of time when consolidating. If you stretch out the payments, you'll end up paying more interest over the life of the loan.

Check out the following sources for student loan consolidation:

The U.S. Education Department, www.loanconsolidation.ed.gov, 800-557-7392. This site has a calculator to help you figure out what your interest rate would be if you consolidate.

Sallie Mae, www.salliemae.com, 800-448-3533

Collegiate Funding, www.collegiatefunding.com, 800-918-7587

College Loan Corp., www.collegeloancorp.com, 800-226-5534

Consolidation is one way to reduce education costs, but don't forget Uncle Sam. You could save some bucks if you qualify for a **tax deduction for the interest you've paid on student loans** this year. The full deductible amount on 2004 returns was $2,500. For married couples filing a joint return, the full deduction could be claimed if your modified adjusted gross income (MAGI) was $100,000 or less. The deduction phased out for those with a MAGI that was more than

$100,000 but less than $130,000. If you are married, you must file a joint tax return to claim this deduction (as opposed to Married, Filing Separate). Normally credit card interest isn't tax deductible. But if you used a credit card exclusively for tuition, fees, books, room and board and you're still paying off the balance, you could deduct the interest if you meet the income requirements.

Other tax savings related to education include:

**Hope Credit.** This is only available if you or your spouse are in your first two years of college. The credit cannot be taken if you claim the tuition and fees deduction, mentioned above. To claim the Hope Credit you have to be enrolled in school at least half-time and you need to be pursuing a degree (as opposed to taking courses for continued education or enrichment). The Hope Credit gives you a tax credit, reducing the amount of tax you have to pay, by up to $1,500 for qualified education expenses. As always, there are income limitations that affect eligibility. The credit was phased out in 2003 if your MAGI was between $83,000 and $103,000—and you have to file a joint return (if married) to claim the credit. Note that if both you and your spouse qualify, you could each claim this credit.

**Lifetime Learning Credit.** This gives lifelong seekers of knowledge a tax credit of up to $2,000 per *return* (not per person, as with the Hope Credit). This credit can be applied to any post-college courses you take, including those geared to help you acquire or improve job skills. You don't need to be pursuing a degree to qualify, either. The same income restrictions as with the Hope Credit apply. Note that you can't take the Lifetime Learning Credit during the same year as the Hope Credit.

# 7. Saving and Investing: The Way to Build Wealth

You may be happy to know that research shows women tend to make better investors than men do. Why? Because women tend to learn more about an investment before they act, so they make better informed, well-considered decisions. They are much less likely to act on a whim, or on a "hot tip" from a coworker or neighbor. This can save women a lot of money and aggravation. Chances are, by the time a "hot tip" wends its way to you or anyone else it's old news. Whatever news was contained in the tip has already affected the price of the stock, so you wouldn't be getting in on the action before everyone else does.

Money advisors sometimes hear from their clients that they are looking for the next hot stock, hoping to make a killing and beat the market. What is "the market," anyway? Simply put, the market is the collective wisdom of thousands of experts who are continually collecting, analyzing and acting on information about public companies and economic conditions. By the time you or I hear news about a company, the company's stock price has already been affected.

All we can reasonably expect from our investments is a return commensurate with the amount of risk we take. Instead of worrying about finding a hot stock or tip, one of the best and most reliable ways to build wealth is by consistently investing over a long period of time so that your money can grow.

There are three main questions to answer when making investment decisions:

1. *Your objectives.* What are you saving for? A house? A vacation? Retirement? A maternity leave? By determining your objectives, you'll know how much you need to save.

2. *Your time frame.* When will you need the money? In one year? Three years? Eight years? Thirty-five years? How long you have to save will help determine where you ought to stash your cash, and it will also help you figure out how much you need to set aside each month to reach your various goals.

3. *Your risk tolerance.* How aggressive are you willing to be when investing for long-term goals? This will help determine your investment choices.

In chapter 5, you and your honey (hopefully) hammered out your money goals, prioritized them and set rough dates by which you hope to achieve them. Later in this chapter we'll discuss risk tolerance and asset allocation. I will also include a tragic, cautionary tale, starring myself, called "How to Lose Almost All the Money in Your IRA Without Really Trying."

Before we get started, it's important to understand the difference between saving and investing. Saving is for fairly immediate goals, like a car down payment or your next vacation. The money is kept where it is easily accessible and there is little to no risk of losing the principal. Your money won't grow much, but that's the trade-off

114

when you park it someplace that safe. Examples of good savings instruments include a savings or money market account, a money market mutual fund or a Certificate of Deposit.

When you invest, on the other hand, you take more risk to reach a long-term goal, such as saving enough to fund retirement or a child's college education. Investing means putting money into the stock or bond markets, whether it's through a mutual fund or individual stocks or bonds. You stand to lose more when you invest in stocks, but you stand to gain more as well: Historically, large U.S. company stocks have returned an average 11 percent each year, which is more than you can expect from bonds or cash over the long term. Bonds historically return a little under 6 percent annually. So why invest in bonds? For diversification and to buffer the blow when stocks are down.

## Basic Money Facts

There are three basic asset classes that investments fall into.

## Cash and Cash Equivalents

This is where you'll want to save for **short-term goals**—that is, money you'll need in **one to three years**, including your **emergency fund**. These investments are safe in the sense that there is no price fluctuation and you don't risk losing any of the principal. They are *not* safe in the sense that you stand to lose purchasing power. At the interest rates currently paid (between less than 1 percent and 3 percent) you're not even beating the annual inflation rate of 2.7 percent. Still, as a place to keep money accessible, they are the way to go.

When you invest in cash equivalents, your money is typically in a **savings account** or **money market account** (MMA) in a bank, credit union or other Federal Deposit Insurance (FDIC)–insured (up to

$100,000) financial institution. The MMA pays a little higher interest than savings accounts typically do. To find the best rates on money market accounts in your area, check www.bankrate.com. Some internet banks, such as Ing Direct (www.ingdirect.com) offer a higher interest rate than many bricks and mortar banks (2.20 percent at press time) and are able to do so due to low overhead. When researching MMAs, be sure to understand the minimum balance needed to earn the highest interest rate touted. Some banks reserve their highest rates for accounts with balances of $25,000 or more. MMAs have a check-writing component; you're limited to six transfers in a given

## SAMPLE: LOW-COST MONEY MARKET MUTUAL FUNDS

| FUND NAME | MINIMUM INITIAL INVESTMENT | MINIMUM ADDITIONAL INVESTMENT | MINIMUM FOR CHECK-WRITING | EXPENSE RATIO (9/04) |
|---|---|---|---|---|
| Vanguard Prime MF www.vanguard.com 800-662-7447 | $3,000 | $50* | $250 | 0.32% |
| Fidelity US Govt. Reserves www.fidelity.com 800-343-3548 | $2,500 | $100* | $500 | 0.34% |
| TIAA-CREF Money Market Fund www.tiaa-cref.org 800-223-1200 | $2,500 | $50* | $250 | 0.29% |

*if Automatic Investing

month (only three can be checks) without incurring a fee.

Another option is a **money market mutual fund.** These are offered by mutual fund companies, not banks, and thus carry no FDIC insurance. You can write checks against your account, but there's usually a minimum of $100 or more. These funds invest in short-term debt (IOUs issued by corporations and federal, state and local governments) and are considered quite stable. They pay better interest than you'll get from most bank savings or money market accounts, but less than a CD or a bond. The problem with money market mutual funds is that the annual fee and expenses paid for the management of the fund can eat away at your earnings. Thus, if you go this route, make sure you select a fund with low expenses. You can research such funds at www.bankrate.com.

## Fixed Income

When you buy a bond, you lend money to a corporation or government which, in exchange, agrees to repay the amount loaned at a predetermined time (the maturity date). In addition, the issuer agrees to pay a fixed amount of interest for the privilege of borrowing your money. Bonds are issued by corporations (to raise funds to improve or expand the business), municipalities (to raise money for roads, schools, etc.) and the government (called Treasury bills, notes and bonds). They are considered a relatively safe investment, although there are risks involved: interest rate risk, prepayment risk and credit risk.

In terms of interest rate risk, you can lose money on a bond, for example, if it is sold before maturity and interest rates have gone up since you bought it. Why? Let's say you buy a bond that pays 5 percent interest. Interest rates go up, and now someone could buy a bond just like yours, only at a higher interest rate—let's say 7 percent. If you need to sell, no one will want to pay full value for your bond since it's only paying 5 percent. You'd either need to hold onto the bond until maturity to get all of your money back, or recognize that you won't be paid its full value if you sell. In prepayment risk, you could also lose money if the issuer pays back the principal before the maturity date—which could happen in a declining interest rate market. Let's say you buy a bond that pays 5 percent interest and interest rates decline. The issuer would rather pay you back in full and issue a new bond that pays only, say, 3 percent interest. You would then have to reinvest your money at a lower interest rate. The third risk—credit risk—has to do with a bond's credit rating. Every bond is rated by a credit rating company, like Moody's or Standard & Poor's. Ratings range from AAA for the highest rated, lowest risk bonds, down to C or D for the lowest rated, highest risk bonds. A high rating lets investors know that that the issuing government or corporation is likely to meet its obligations. Bonds can lose money if the issuer's credit rating goes south (suggesting there is a chance the issuer can't repay the principal and interest). If you wanted to sell, you wouldn't get the full value because of the bond's lousy credit rating. (As in, who wants your crummy bond that the issuer might default on anyway?) Worse still, the issuer could actually default on the loan and you could lose your investment altogether.

In spite of the risks—and they can be managed in part by only buying bonds rated A or higher—bonds are a necessary part of any long-term investment portfolio. They provide diversification—typically when stocks are down, bonds are up. And even though there are risks, bonds are much less volatile than stocks. It is unlikely, however, at this stage of your investment life that you will invest in individual bonds. Your exposure will come through bond mutual funds, which will be further discussed under Mutual Funds, below.

The one fixed income asset you *can* use now is **Certificates of Deposit** (CDs), which are suited for reaching short-term goals like a house or car down payment. (Note: Don't put your emergency fund in CDs; they are not liquid enough.) These savings instruments pay better interest than you can expect from a savings or money market account. How much better depends on how long you hold the CD— **the longer it takes to reach the maturity date, the better the yield.** CDs can be bought at a bank or savings institution or from a broker, and they are covered by FDIC up to $100,000. The way they work is you invest a fixed amount of money for a specific period of time— for example, three months, six months, one year, two years or more. Typically you get your money back, with interest, when you cash in the CD. (These days, however, some longer-term CDs of three years or more let you elect to have the interest credited to your bank account every quarter or six months.) If you cash in the CD before the maturity date, you'll either pay an early withdrawal penalty or you'll lose some interest. If you're using CDs to meet a money goal, remember that interest earned is taxable at your tax rate (e.g., if you're in the 25 percent tax bracket, you'll lose 25 percent of your earnings to Uncle Sam, so you'll need to earn that much more to make up for it).

CDs used to be pretty straightforward, but banks have added features to try to make them more attractive to customers. At one time CDs only had fixed rates, but now the rate could be fixed or variable. Also, there are "liquid" CDs that let you withdraw your money early without penalty (you won't get as high an interest rate at the outset), and "bump-up" CDs that let you capture a higher interest rate if rates go up before your CD matures. But the latter is for a sophisticated investor who not only keeps a close watch on interest rates, but has a strong opinion about where rates are going. Thus, if you simply want to put some money in a safe place, collect some interest and forget about it, the bump-up isn't for you.

Three basic things to know when you buy a CD are 1.) the maturity date 2.) how much interest you'll be paid and 3.) when. If you have a few thousand dollars saved and don't need the money all at once, consider "laddering" CDs by buying a few with different maturity rates. The longer the term, the more interest you can earn. For example, at current rates you could buy a six-month CD earning 1.48 percent interest. But if you didn't need all the money right away, you could buy an eighteen-month CD throwing off 2.83 percent interest. Be sure to shop around, starting with your own bank. Also check www.bankrate.com for CD rates.

## COMPOUND INTEREST: A BORING WAY OF SAYING, FREE MONEY!

What is compound interest, anyway? Simply put, compound interest means you earn interest on the original amount that you've invested, and then you earn interest on the interest. You didn't even have to bust your hump in the office to get it. (As you're probably aware, that's one of the ways rich people live—off the earnings of the principal they have invested.)

Of course, the earlier you start saving for goals, the less you'll have to save—the interest will do some of the job for you. For example, let's say you invest $2,000 at a rate of return of 5 percent. After the first year, you will have $2,100. The following year you're earning interest not on $2,000, but on $2,100. Your money continues to grow year after year, with earnings building on earnings. If you want to experiment with how much you need to save each month at various rates of return to meet various money goals, check out the savings calculator at www.quicken.com (see "Tools" under Bills and Banking).

## Stock or Equities

If you have time for your money to work—meaning at least five years—you'll want to invest it where you can make it grow as much as possible, and that means investing in stocks. You buy stock in publicly traded companies; each share you buy is one unit of ownership. If you were to buy individual stocks, you could do so through a stockbroker or, even better, a discount brokerage to cut commission costs (however, a discount brokerage wouldn't give you the advice and handholding a full-service broker would). Unless you have the time and inclination to consistently study and track the companies you're interested in and invest in (you should never just hand your money over to someone to invest for you and not stay involved in what is happening with it), you're better off buying stocks via various types of mutual funds.

## Investing in Mutual Funds

Mutual funds are perfect for people who want to invest in stocks and bonds, but who don't want the hassle of making the selections themselves. The funds are professionally managed, and while you, as a shareholder, do pay fees and possibly sales charges for the management of the fund, it is a less expensive way of investing than if you worked with an individual stockbroker or other commissioned money advisor.

When you invest in a mutual fund, you pool your money with thousands of other people who have paid into the fund. Each fund has its own investment objective. It is the fund manager's responsibility to determine how to invest shareholders' money in a way that best meets those objectives. Another advantage to mutual funds is the diversification they provide. For example, instead of owning just one or two

121

individual stocks, a stock fund holds many, even hundreds. This reduces risk since your money isn't all riding on the fortunes of one or two companies. Mutual fund companies typically offer a wide selection of funds from which to choose, which is why such a company might be referred to as a family of funds. At this stage in your investing life, you're most apt to come in contact with mutual funds via your 401(k) plan. It's good, then, to familiarize yourself with the basics. There are five main types of funds:

Equity funds: Invest in stocks of U.S. or foreign companies.

Bond funds: Invest in bonds of all types.

Balanced, or hybrid, funds: Invest in a combination of stocks and bonds.

Real estate funds: Invest in companies that build or invest in various types of real estate.

Money market funds: Invest in low-risk, short-term debt of corporations and governments, like Treasury bills and commercial paper. As mentioned earlier, these can be a good parking place for emergency funds if the expenses aren't high.

## Stock Funds

Of course, all stock funds aren't alike, nor are all bond funds. Stock funds vary in two ways: by investing philosophy and by size of the company that the money is invested in.

### INVESTING STRATEGY

*Growth funds:* These funds invest in companies whose stock is expected to appreciate due to the earnings growth of the company. Because these are elite companies—blue chips, such as IBM—the stock price is often high (and could precipitously fall at any moment). For that reason, growth stocks are considered risky investments.

*Value funds:* Value stocks, on the other hand, represent weaker companies. Because these are lower-quality companies, there is less interest in them and the stock price isn't inflated. Such companies are attractive to investors because if the company improves its prospects, the investor can achieve outsize gains.

*Blend funds:* These funds invest in a combination of growth and value stocks.

*Balanced (or hybrid) funds:* Invest in stocks and bonds.

*Growth and income funds:* Invest in companies that are expected to grow, balanced by companies that pay a dividend (considered "income").

*Equity income funds:* Primarily invest in stocks that pay dividends.

## BY COMPANY SIZE

*Large-cap funds:* These funds tend to be populated by large, established companies like the Microsofts of the world. And size does matter: The companies in large-cap funds have market value of more than $9 billion. (In case you're wondering, "cap" is short for capitalization, as in market capitalization. It refers to the value of the shareholders ownership in the company.)

*Mid-cap funds:* As the name implies, these funds focus on medium-size companies. Their market value ranges from $1 billion to $9 billion.

*Small-cap funds:* These focus on stocks of emerging companies with a market value of less than $1 billion.

## INTERNATIONAL FUNDS

As the name implies, international funds invest in companies outside of the United States. The fund might focus on one country or region, or simply hold the stock of a variety of foreign companies. Global funds invest in both U.S. and foreign stocks.

## INDEX FUNDS

Index funds are mutual funds that mimic the performance of a stock market index, such as the S&P 500, the Russell 2000 or the Wilshire 5000. These funds hold all, or a representative sample, of stocks in the index it is tracking. (There are also bond index funds, which track the U.S. bond market.) There is a very compelling reason why you should consider index funds for your portfolio: Over the long term, the S&P 500 index beats the returns of 80 percent of actively managed funds! In addition, since the funds are not actively managed (there is no expensive fund manager or analyst to hire), the expenses you pay are much lower—they could be as low as .18 percent versus 3 percent for a managed fund. Index funds are also considered tax efficient. Each year mutual funds are required to pay capital gains—when you make money, you know Uncle Sam can't be far behind looking for his cut. But the stocks in an index fund aren't constantly traded, so there are fewer transactions that result in capital gains that must be taxed each year.

There are other types of funds I left out (for example sector funds, which focus on one industry and thus are considered less diversified). The ones we've discussed are the kind you'll most likely find offered in your 401(k), or that you will select from for an IRA. If your 401(k) is lacking a fund category you're interested in—such as an index fund—it is worthwhile to talk to your HR administrator about the possibility of having such a fund added to the mix.

## Bond Funds

Bonds are considered much less volatile than stocks and, as such, should be part of any investment portfolio. Bond funds invest in a pool of bonds, such as municipal, corporate and U.S. government bonds, or foreign bonds. Bonds are also classified by the maturity date by which the borrower (i.e., the government or corporation) needs to pay the money back. Such bonds are referred to as short-term, intermediate-term and long-term bond funds.

There are tips below for selecting mutual funds. When selecting a bond fund, however, there are a couple of additional factors to pay attention to:

- Consider the bond fund's average maturity. Stick with funds with short (five years or less) or intermediate maturity dates (five to ten years). Funds with long maturities are much riskier, but the potential reward isn't there.

- Consider the average bond rating of the fund. Choose funds with a rating of AA or better.

How much money should you invest in the more staid bond funds? One rule of thumb is to invest a percentage equal to your age. So if you're 28, you would allocate 28 percent of your portfolio to bond funds. (A more conservative investor, however, would increase that amount to 35 or 40 percent.)

> ## KNOW YOUR NAV
>
> When you want to buy—or sell—shares in a mutual fund, how is the price per share (known as the NAV, or Net Asset Value) determined? At the end of each business day, fund administrators add up the market value of the fund's investments. They then subtract the fund's liabilities (debts) and divide that figure by the total number of outstanding shares to get the NAV.

## Choosing a Mutual Fund

With about 8,300 funds to choose from, the prospect of making a few smart choices can seem overwhelming. But once you start to compare key factors in funds, you can weed out the bad ones pretty quickly. There are a variety of factors to consider that need to be taken into consideration together. You can't just look at recent returns to know if a fund is the right one for your portfolio. You can find very thorough research of funds at www.morningstar.com, which also rates funds on a scale of one to five. While independent analysis is important, you can also call a fund's 800 number to get the answers to some of the questions below, such as fees, how long the fund manager has been in place, etc. It's also important to read a fund's prospectus before investing; it will contain a lot of information about expenses, performance history and investing philosophy. Generally speaking, this is what to hone in on when considering a fund:

1. Rate of return. The rate posted is after expenses have been deducted. Obviously, the higher the better. However, it would be a mistake to look at funds that did great in the last year and simply

buy those without looking at all the other factors. Last year's leading fund could be this year's loser.

2. Volatility. How volatile is the fund apt to be? You can tell by looking at the fund's past performance over several years. Has it been a pretty steady performer, or does it reflect dramatic losses and gains? However the fund has performed, you should expect more of the same. With that as a given, decide what kind of ride you want to take with your money. Suppose there was a year when the fund lost 30 percent. Would you be able to stomach watching your account balance dip by that much, or would you feel compelled to sell? Ideally, you want to make selections you can buy and hold for a long time. If you can't take downs that are that dramatic, look for a less volatile fund.

3. Management of the fund. How long has the manager been in place? Look at the five- or ten-year returns of the fund. Are they favorable? If so, was the current manager at the fund when those returns were realized?

4. Performance. How has the fund performed compared to other funds of its kind, over the same time period? It should at least be in the top quartile.

5. Cost of investing. Is there a sales charge when you buy into the fund or when you sell your shares? (Avoid such funds.) What does the fund charge in fees and expenses? (Unavoidable, but you can pick a fund with low expenses.) These costs eat away at your returns.

6. What is the fund's stated investment strategy and objective? Read the prospectus—then decide if the fund fills a need in your portfolio.

## FEE FOLLY

If you buy a mutual fund from a stockbroker or other commissioned money advisor, you pay for his or her advice via a sales charge, or "load," which is typically 3 to 5 percent of your investment. (Note: These money advisors may also receive commissions from the mutual funds they recommend. It's up to you to decide how objective they are apt to be.) The following fees will be listed in the prospectus under "Shareholder Fees."

*Front load:* This is the amount paid when you first invest in the fund. Let's say a fund has a 5 percent front-end load. If you write a check to the fund for $2,000, the sales load would be $100, which is deducted from your check and paid to the broker who sold you the fund. The remaining $1,900 is invested. Mutual funds with front loads are usually called A-class shares.

*Back-end load:* Instead of paying a sales charge when you buy into the fund, you pay one to the broker when you sell it. The back-end load is calculated on the lesser of your original investment and the account balance when you sell. If you invested $1,000 and your balance is $1,300 when you sell, the back-end load would be based on $1,000. If you move your money to a different fund within the same fund family, you may be able to avoid a back-end fee. These are called B-class shares.

*Deferred sales charge (load):* This is a back-end load that goes away if you hold onto your shares for a long enough period of time. For example, if you sell your shares within a year of purchase, the deferred sales load might be 5 percent; if you sell within two years it's 4 percent, until it trends down to zero. These are called C-class shares.

*12b-1 fee:* This is an annual 1 percent fee paid by you for the fund to market (advertise/sell/push) its shares. This fee exists whenever there is a back-end load.

Funds also have operating expenses. They are paid out of fund assets, and as such shareholders pay these expenses indirectly. It's important to be aware of a fund's expenses before you invest, since fees and expenses impact your return. Such costs are listed in the prospectus under a fee table. As you compare funds, compare the expenses that are charged. For example, there may be a purchase fee that the fund is paid when you buy in, a redemption fee when you sell shares, a management fee that goes to the fund's investment adviser, etc. The main figure to look at in the fee table is the Total Annual Fund Operating Expenses, called the Expense Ratio. This is the total of the fund's operating expenses, stated as a percentage of the fund's average net assets. Naturally, the lower the Expense Ratio, the better.

The best way to get the most bang from your investing buck is to buy directly from a mutual fund company and invest in *no-load funds*. There are fees attached to these funds, of course, since it takes a certain amount of money to run the fund, but the fees are less than if you purchased shares in a fund with a sales load. Two solid fund families to consider with no-load funds are Vanguard and Fidelity. Sometimes commissioned money advisors offer to buy you into a no-load fund. They may not charge you a load, but they'll charge you an annual fee, which would be 1 percent to 1.5 percent of the total amount invested. Better to pick your own funds and let more of your money go to work for you. If you do feel you need advice, consider the services of a fee-only financial planner. Check the National Association of Personal Finance Advisors (www.napfa.org), a trade group for fee-only advisors, to locate one in your area. Such advisors do not receive commissions from mutual funds, so you know their advice is not based on who pays them to recommend certain funds.

## Know Your Risk Tolerance

What if you woke up one morning and discovered that one of your mutual funds had lost half of its value? Would your stomach churn? Would you look like the figure in the famous Edvard Munch painting, *The Scream*? Or would you take it in stride (sort of ), figure time is on your side and that you'll make up your losses? There are varying degrees of risk tolerance. Which best describes you?

Conservative: You're willing to take very little risk in exchange for very modest returns.

Moderate conservative: You're willing to take a little bit of risk for slightly better returns.

Moderate: You're willing to assume average risk for average returns.

Moderate aggressive: You're willing to take higher risk for potentially higher returns.

Aggressive: You're ready to bet the farm. You're willing to take enormous risk for potentially big returns, realizing also that if the market goes south you face the risk of substantial losses.

Naturally, everyone wants to make a lot of money from their investments. But the more aggressively you invest, the more risk you will need to take. In the end, you'll want to make choices that leave room for making gains with your investments, but still allow you to sleep at night.

## Dollar Cost Average Your Way to Wealth

One of the best ways to invest in mutual funds is a strategy called dollar cost averaging. The idea is pretty simple, and if you have a 401(k) plan you've invested in automatically, you're already doing it. Basically it means you invest a set amount in regular intervals (e.g., monthly), no matter what the market is doing. Thus, when the price per share of your mutual fund is down, you buy more shares than when the price is up. The net result is that you accumulate shares at an average price, gradually, which is better than buying them all at once, at a high price. Naturally, we would all prefer to buy when prices are low, but since it's impossible to time the market, this is the next best thing.

## How Fast Can You Double Your Money?

Here's a fun fact that will perhaps inspire you to keep socking away money: The Rule of 72. Here's how it works. Take the amount you think your money can earn each year. Let's be conservative and say 8 percent. Divide that amount into 72, and that's how long it will take you to double your money, assuming 8 percent interest is paid every year and that the earnings are reinvested. In this example, 72 divided by 8 equals 9—it would take 9 years to double your money. Let's say you've invested $10,000 and you figure you'll earn a 10 percent return. Using our handy calculation (72 divided by 10) you'll have $20,000 in 7.2 years. The mathematical equation works. The tricky part comes in guessing how much your money will actually return. Some years you may earn more than 10 percent, some years less. But it's a good rule to bear in mind when you're weighing whether or not to throw an extra $100 a month into your 401(k) the next time you get a raise. Just think about doubling that money!

## Two Things That Suck and Hurt Your Returns

The first is inflation. As you know, the cost of things keep going up. As a result, the money you earn today will have less purchasing power tomorrow. What does that translate to in everyday life? Consider that the current inflation rate is 2.7 percent, according to the Bureau of Labor Statistics (and that's bound to change by the time you read this). So let's say you have $3,000 in a money market mutual fund earning only 1 percent interest—a typical yield at today's rates. After one year you've earned $30. But the 2.7 percent inflation rate erodes that by 81 cents, leaving you with $29.19. Inflation is also working on your original $3,000 investment, which a year later is worth $2,919. In the end your account balance reads $3,030, but you only have $2,948.19 in actual purchasing power. This is why it's so important for your returns to at least keep pace with the inflation rate. The other fact of the financial life that messes with your returns is—need I say it—taxes. The best thing you can do for now is to sock as much money as you can into tax-deferred retirement accounts, such as your 401(k) and IRAs, if you qualify for the tax deduction. You will pay taxes on the money, but that's years away. When you get into the higher income brackets and are also investing outside of tax-deferred savings plans, consult with your accountant for investment choices that will help manage the tax bite.

## How Do Funds Make You Money?

There are three basic ways.

1. Dividend payments. A stock in the fund may pay dividends, or you may earn interest on a security in the portfolio. This money gets paid to shareholders minus expenses.

2. Capital gains distributions. The price of securities in the fund may increase. When the fund sells that stock, the fund has a

capital gain. These are distributed to shareholders at the end of the year, minus any capital losses.

3. Increased NAV. This is the case if the market value of the fund's portfolio increases after subtracting expenses and liabilities.

Funds give shareholders the option to receive dividend payments and capital gains distributions in a check, or to have the money reinvested in the fund (the wealth-building choice!).

## Asset Allocation

I am writing this from the perspective that you are primarily concerned with using mutual funds to invest money for the long-term, i.e., retirement. Whether you're making choices for a 401(k) plan or an IRA, you'll need to decide (or perhaps you're reviewing) how your money is invested. The idea is to be properly diversified between investments that run the spectrum, from aggressive to safe. It's the "don't put all of your eggs in one basket" approach. After all, look at what happened to the Enron employees who put all of their retirement savings into company stock! Ouch. If company stock is part of your 401(k) menu of choices, limit it to 10 or 20 percent of your account's value to avoid getting burned should things go . . . er . . . badly. If you need to invest in company stock to get a company match, only put in as much as you have to to get the match.

What follows is one suggested mix for an investor in her twenties or thirties who is saving for retirement in a 401(k):

Strategic Asset Allocation

Small-cap stocks . . . . . . . . . . . . . . . . . . . . . . . . .15%

Mid-cap stocks . . . . . . . . . . . . . . . . . . . . . . . . . .10%

Large-cap stocks . . . . . . . . . . . . . . . . . . . . . . . .25%

International stocks . . . . . . . . . . . . . . . . . . . . . .20%

Real Estate Investment Trust (REIT) . . . . . . . . . .5%

Short-term bonds . . . . . . . . . . . . . . . . . . . . . . . . .5%

Intermediate-term bonds . . . . . . . . . . . . . . . . . .5%

High-yield bonds . . . . . . . . . . . . . . . . . . . . . . . .10%

Money Market . . . . . . . . . . . . . . . . . . . . . . . . . . .5%

*Source: L.J. Alfest & Co.*

As you can see, with such a diverse allocation your money would be spread around enough so that if you took a hit in one fund, you'd have several others to soften the blow. Several types of stock funds are included simply to reduce risk—not every business is going to fare poorly at the same time, and general economic developments won't hit every sector in the same way. The bond funds are diversified by maturity dates.

It's difficult to make one recommendation that fits everyone's taste and risk tolerance (and it also depends, of course, on what your 401(k) actually offers) but the above gives you a guideline for a well-diversified portfolio. "Some people don't mind seeing their portfolio fluctuate a lot, while others are more conservative," notes Andrew Altfest, an advisor with L. J. Alfest & Co., a fee-only financial planning firm in New York City. For investors in their twenties and thirties, "We stress that they should have at least 65 percent in stocks and 35 percent in bonds/cash in their 401(k)," he says. He further notes that for those who could stand the fluctuation, "Even 85 percent in stocks and 15 percent in bonds wouldn't be outrageous."

Suppose, however, you are just starting out and putting money into an IRA. You wouldn't need to spread a small amount of money over so many funds. In that case, consider putting your money into an index fund, such as Vanguard S&P 500, recommends Victoria Collins, CFP, executive vice president with The Keller Group in Irvine, California. "This gives the investor full diversification with one fund," she says. "It's not actively managed and costs are low. It's a good place to start and get exposure to the stock market." Not only that, but you don't have to track performance and worry about whether the manager is doing a good job, since the fund automatically tracks the market as a whole. Once you build up your account to $10,000 or so, you can start to diversify so that you would have 60 percent in the S&P index fund, 20 percent in an international fund and 20 percent in a bond fund, notes Collins. As your accounts grow you'll want to continue to diversify, moving closer to the model above.

## Another Asset Allocation View

There is an excellent book you must read that explains why investors are best off simply investing in a mix of index funds. It's not a beach book, but as investment books go, this one's actually a pretty interesting—and fast—read. It's called *The Random Walk Guide to Investing: Ten Rules for Financial Success* by Burton G. Malkiel, who is a professor of economics at Princeton University. In a nutshell, this is what Professor Malkiel recommends for those investing in tax-advantaged retirement plans, such as a 401(k), IRA, etc.:

1. Invest in index funds because, generally speaking, they outperform actively managed funds. For further diversification between asset classes, invest in a stock, bond and real estate index fund. There are hundreds to pick from, so you still have to do your due diligence reevaluating performance and costs associated with the fund.

2. Buy a single stock fund that buys and holds all the stocks in the market. Such funds, typically called "Total Stock Market" funds, invest in both large companies and small, value and growth stocks across all industry groups. Professor Malkiel recommends buying an index fund that tracks either the Wilshire 5000-Total Stock Market Index or the Russell 3000 Index. As mentioned previously, always look for a low Expense Ratio and a no-load fund. Two he cites include Vanguard Total Stock Market Index, which tracks the Wilshire 5000 (www.vanguard.com) 800-662-7447 and TIAA-CREF Equity Index Fund (www.tiaa-cref.org) 800-842-1924, which tracks the Russell 3000 index.

3. Buy a bond fund index, which holds a wide selection of corporate and government bonds. Again: Keep your costs down. Pick one with a low Expense Ratio and no load. A couple of Malkiel's picks include USAA Income Fund (www.usaa.com) 800-531-8181 and Vanguard Total Bond Market Index Fund (www.vanguard.com) 800-662-7447.

4. Get exposure to the real estate market through a REIT index fund. These funds invest in various types of properties (residential and commercial) in different regions of the country. Again, diversification is the key. You want to pick an index fund that includes a portfolio of REITs that is diversified by geographic area and property type. Two Professor Malkiel recommends include Vanguard REIT Index Fund (www.vanguard.com) 800-662-7447 and TIAA-CREF Real Estate Securities Fund (www.tiaa-cref.org) 800-842-1924.

What about asset allocation for a twentysomething? His recommendations are in line with the others, as noted above: 65 percent in stocks, 20 percent in bonds, 10 percent in real estate and 5 percent in cash (money market fund).

## Rebalance Your Portfolio

Once a year, you should review your portfolio and rebalance it, if necessary. What does that mean? Due to the gains and losses your funds have realized throughout the year, your asset allocation could be out of whack. Maybe you want 70 percent in stocks and 20 percent in bonds, and now you've got 80 percent in stocks. Your portfolio is now riskier than what you originally planned for it to be. Rebalancing is simple. You could simply move some of the money in the overweighted stock fund into one of the bond funds. Or you could put your new contributions into the bond fund. That way you'll move back to your original asset allocation.

## Evaluate Your Portfolio

In addition to rebalancing your portfolio, you'll want to review your mutual funds' performances once a year. If a fund's performance is lagging, review the following:

- Has management changed?

- Compare the fund's performance to others of its kind on Morningstar. Is it in the bottom half of the rankings compared to its peers?

- Has the investment style changed? Perhaps you bought a large-cap value fund that is now a growth fund.

You probably wouldn't want to sell the first time there is a dip in earnings, but if the fund has switched its objectives or has a new manager who isn't delivering as well as the previous one, consider making a change. If nothing fundamental about the fund has changed except the fact that earnings are down, follow its performance for another six to twelve months. If it continues to lag, you may want to start looking into other funds of its kind.

## How to Lose Almost All the Money in Your IRA without Really Trying

If this were a play, it would be a tragedy, and no, it wouldn't be a comic tragedy because hey, I'm not laughing. Here's my sad story: I started out with $74,981.18 in my IRA in February of 2000. By September of 2004, I had $19,635.00. What happened, and why? I share my story in the hopes that it will save a few of you from making some of the same mistakes I made.

At various family gatherings, my Uncle Wally (not his real name), a stockbroker, regaled me from time to time with his investing conquests. I mostly tuned out the chatter. But, like any good salesperson, he kept it up. I got the hint. He wanted to manage my IRA money, which I revealed I had. It was the late nineties when this subtle sales pitch was going on, and the stock market was surging. People were making money left and right. It's a period of what Federal Reserve Chairman Alan Greenspan called "irrational exuberance," a phrase he used in late 1996 to describe the overvalued market of the time. In other words, stock prices, especially of tech companies, kept going up, regardless of the company's underlying value, or lack thereof. My money was invested in a boring old mutual fund. Meanwhile, I kept hearing about all the money people were making in the stock market. And along came Uncle Wally, with the promise of a much better return on my money. As fate would have it, in April of 2000 I finally rolled my IRA account into the brokerage firm of Wally (Score!). He promptly bought me the hot stocks of the moment, like Cisco, Global Crossing, and Nokia, at their most expensive. Now, of course neither he, nor I, knew these stocks were going to begin to lose value and not recover. What we'd been seeing was wild dips in the market—stocks gaining value, losing it, then gaining it again all in the space of an hour or a day or a week. But as it turned out, I bought in at the peak, and then the stock market began a downward slide from which it didn't begin to recover until three years later. And I lost $55,346.18.

Long-term investors would say, What's the big deal? Anyone invested in stocks during that time period lost money (true). If you're in it for the long run, you're supposed to stay invested and ride it out. Yes, true. But I made some mistakes that I think are worth passing on. I might add that Uncle Wally was doing exactly what a lot of other stockbrokers and money advisors and investors were doing at the time, so it's not like we were off on some weird tangent. (So much for following the crowd, huh?) Here is what you should *not* do when it comes to investing your money:

1. Do not hand your money over to just anyone, trusting that he or she will take care of you. Perhaps many of us, on some deep level, would like nothing more than to hand responsibility for some aspect of our lives—like our finances—over to someone else. Wrong! Relinquishing responsibility is never a good idea—it robs you of your power, and if things don't work out, it leaves you pissed off. If you are going to work one-on-one with an advisor of any type—even a relative—you must stay involved and actively participate in the decisions being made.

2. Understand how your money is being invested, and what the up and down side is to that investment strategy. When I turned my account over to Wally, we did not have a conversation about the overall strategy, or how much risk I wanted to take. Yes, he probably should have asked me, but I'm not going to pass the

buck. I should have asked him about his plan for my money. As I was working on this book, I went through my brokerage file containing all the statements. Stuck in the back was an account agreement form. I'm certain that when this arrived in the mail I simply stuffed it into the file without even looking at it. Too bad for me. Under "Investment Objectives," Wally had checked "Income, Growth & Speculation." Speculation?! I've never been that much of a high flier. If I had seen it, I would like to think that I would have at least questioned it and asked what it meant—and perhaps put the brakes on buying some of the riskier stocks.

3. Be properly diversified. I only held a handful of stocks in my IRA, and they were mostly in technology. That is nuts. Very little in cash, no bonds and no protection from what happened when the market dipped—and stayed there. I have now gone back to a mutual fund, and am invested in Vanguard STAR fund, which is a balanced fund. If the market surges I may not capture the highest of the returns, but I also won't get slaughtered when the market comes back to earth, as it always does.

4. Stick to mutual funds. Unless you have the time to really watch your investments (rule #1), you're best off with the professional management of a no-load mutual fund.

The things I learned aren't startlingly new lessons in the world of finance. In fact, I did know, in theory anyway, about diversification, and risk tolerance, etc., since I had written on these topics in the past. Unfortunately, I didn't apply them to my own life when it mattered. If you don't repeat my mistakes, it may be worth the $55,346.18 it cost me to learn them!

# 8. Buying a Home, Sweet Home

Buying a home is often at the top of most newlyweds' list, as it well should be. Home ownership gives you an important tax break since you can deduct mortgage interest and property taxes, it provides a sense of security and stability and gives you a chance to make a home—decorated to your liking—for your future family. Owning your own home is also an important part of retirement planning. Ideally you'll have a place to live mortgage-free by the time you're ready to quit working, or at the least you'll have a valuable asset to sell and make part of your nest egg.

But buying a home is a huge financial undertaking. It's important to go in aware of all the costs involved so that you can take this step when you are truly ready. Buying—and then having to sell your house because you can't afford it—would not only be disappointing, but an expensive proposition. In this chapter we'll discuss all the basics of home ownership, from knowing when you're ready to buy, to shopping for a house and a mortgage, to closing on your dream house. Whether you decide to buy now or in a year or so, this chapter will bring you up to speed on what you need to know to be a savvy consumer.

## Should You Buy or Rent?

Most everyone wants to own their own place—home ownership still defines a large part of the American dream. But that doesn't mean you have to rush into buying a home before you're ready. The fact is, owning a home can cost considerably more than renting an apartment. It's not just a question of coming up with a down payment (though these days you can get a mortgage with zero down). There are closing costs, which run around 1 to 3 percent of the purchase price. Yes, those could also be folded into the mortgage, or you could even get the seller to kick in the money to cover the closing costs. Still, once you're in the house, you need to be able to pay the mortgage plus taxes, utilities, maintenance (you should budget 1 percent of the cost of the house for maintenance each year) repairs, homeowner's insurance, water and garbage pick-up, to name a few. If you have never paid for utilities, for example, you could be in for a shock when you discover that on top of the mortgage payment you're shelling out $200 to $300 a month or more for gas and electric, depending, of course, on the season, the size of your house and where you live. That said, here are the general pros and cons of buying versus renting:

Clearly buying holds many advantages, and the question to be asked isn't really if you should buy, but when. The primary reason not to buy, as indicated in the chart above, is if you can't currently afford all of the attendant costs that come with home ownership—or, for example, if you're in a highly priced market where it's difficult to find anything affordable. Another reason not to buy immediately is if you're not sure where you want to live or if you anticipate a transfer. Selling a house is expensive—you need to pay a real estate agent a commission, on average, of 6 percent, plus seller's closing costs, which could come to about 1½ percent of the sale price. Your house may not gain enough value to cover those costs if you buy and sell

| | PROS OF BUYING | PROS OF RENTING |
|---|---|---|
| **PROS** | You're forced to save, building equity in something that appreciates in value<br><br>Mortgage interest and real estate taxes are tax-deductible if you itemize deductions<br><br>Inspires stronger sense of belonging to a community<br><br>You can decorate and landscape as you please | You're not responsible for maintenance/repairs<br><br>You can move at the drop of a hat<br><br>Money saved from costs associated with home ownership can be invested and potentially earn a higher rate of return |
| **CONS** | You have to physically maintain the property<br><br>Cost of maintenance, utilities, taxes<br><br>Costs related to buying/selling can be high<br><br>Possibility of foreclosure if you hit on financial hard times | No tax benefits<br><br>Regular rent increases<br><br>You own nothing of increasing value<br><br>Possibility of eviction |

quickly. (Houses typically gain between 3 and 5 percent in value each year, although in some hot markets it can be considerably higher, say 20 percent or more.) Generally speaking, buy with the idea that you'll stay put for at least three to five years. From a tax standpoint, living in the house for at least two of five years of ownership also means that if you sell, you can avoid paying taxes on capital gains of up to $500,000 if you and your spouse file a joint return.

## How Much House Can You Afford?

Once you've made the decision to buy, you need to figure out how much of a mortgage you can afford. No point wasting time looking at houses and getting all misty-eyed over homes that are currently out of your reach—and frankly, no real estate agent is going to want to show you around until it's clear what your limits are. Indeed, a good buyer's agent will prequalify you for a mortgage before taking you house-hunting, according to Betty Messman, housing specialist at Consumer Credit Counseling Service in Fort Worth (www.cccsfw.org), which provides, among other things, counseling and educational programs on buying, selling and maintaining homes. Getting prequalified is also a good idea because you may be able to lock in a mortgage rate (ask to get it in writing that you will get a lower rate if it goes down before you close). In addition, getting prequalified makes you more attractive to sellers if they know you'll be able to close without any hitches.

To figure out how much house you can afford, you need to do a couple of simple calculations using two standard debt-to-income ratios. The first, the housing expense, or **front-end ratio**, shows how much of your gross (before tax) income would go to your mortgage payment. Generally speaking, you shouldn't put more than one-third of your gross income into your mortgage payment, which includes the principal, interest, taxes and homeowner's insurance (sometimes referred to as PITI). (If you put less than 20 percent down you'll also have to pay for another type of insurance, called Private Mortgage Insurance, or PMI, which protects the lender in case you default on the loan.) To figure out the maximum you can afford in a monthly payment, multiply your combined household income by 0.33, then divide by twelve (months). Ideally that's the most you would pay for your mortgage each month. Example: Let's say you and your DH have a combined income of $100,000. Using the one-third ratio (multiplying by .33) you shouldn't put more than $33,000 per year ($2,750 per month) into the cost of your mortgage.

The next calculation you need to do is the total debt-to-income, or **back-end ratio**. This indicates how much of your gross income goes to *all* of your debts: your mortgage plus other obligations, such as credit cards, car loans, student loans and personal loans. Experts recommend that this figure not exceed 36 percent of your gross income. Example: You and your DH have a combined income of $100,000. Multiplying by .36, your total monthly obligations (mortgage plus all other debt) should not come to more than $3,000. There is some leeway in these recommendations, based on how much of a down payment you put down. Bob Armbruster, president of the National Association of Mortgage Brokers, suggests the following:

Front-end ratio: Percentage of total house payment to gross income.

Preferred range: 28 percent to 33 percent. The less you put down, the closer you should stick to the lower number. (To do this calculation, multiply gross income by .28 to .33.)

Back-end ratio: Percentage of total house payment plus all debt payments to gross income.

Preferred range: 33 percent to 36 percent. (Multiply gross income by .33 to .36.)

If your debts are high, taking you out of these preferred ranges, you'll likely need to shop for a less expensive home or apartment, otherwise you may find yourselves in over your heads and unable to meet all of your obligations. Obviously, the sooner you can pay down some of that debt the better. (Indeed, you may need to do so to qualify for a mortgage.)

Now that you know how much you can afford, it's important to shop for a mortgage keeping that figure in mind. Mortgage companies routinely approve people for more than they can afford. While it's important to consider the above ratios, consider your net income— that is the reality of what you're bringing home each month. It's up to you and your DH to know what monthly payment fits your budget, and to stick to that.

## Shopoholics: Start Your Engines

Now comes the fun part. It's time for you and your DH to figure out what you are looking for in a home or apartment so you can communicate that to the Realtor or real estate agent with whom you choose to work. Here are key questions to consider:

1. What types of homes are you willing to consider: single family/condo/co-op/townhouse/two-family?

2. What area(s) do you want to live in?

3. How much are you willing to spend?

4. How long do you plan to stay in the home? (This will help determine the type of mortgage you take.) If you are confident that your incomes will increase in the next few years, you could consider pushing yourselves a little for a higher mortgage if you believe you'll be in the house for ten years or more, notes housing specialist Betty Messman.

5. What is the minimum number of bedrooms you need? (Does the house need to accommodate children?)

6. What is the minimum number of bathrooms you need?

7. How large of a house do you want, in terms of square feet?

8. Are you concerned about the school district and, if so, what are your requirements?

9. Are you willing to renovate and, if so, to what extent?

10. Do you need to be near public transportation?

11. In terms of commuting, are there any highways you need to be near?

12. How large of a lot are you interested in? Large (one acre or more) or small (less than an acre)?

13. What features are you looking for in the house? For example, a fireplace, a separate dining room, a family room, hardwood floors, skylights, a finished basement, a den, a garage, a patio/deck/porch?

14. What, besides schools, are important for you to find in the community? (e.g., child-care options, churches/other places of worship, public facilities such as a swimming pool or tennis courts)?

15. How close do you need to be to shopping (supermarkets, a mall)?

Now you're really getting organized! Your next step is to find a real estate agent who can help you find your dream home.

## Interview Real Estate Agents

Once you're ready to shop in earnest, you'll want to **work with an experienced real estate agent or Realtor** (a real estate agent or broker who is affiliated with the National Association of Realtors) who will best represent your interests (that is, buying a great house at the best possible price). Ideally you'll work with a **buyer's agent** to help you get the job done. Your agent will not only show you appropriate properties, but help you get prequalified for a mortgage, help you understand how homes are priced and assist you with a negotiating strategy, from beginning to end. Your agent will also tell you about any problems with properties you look at (such as a leaky roof), and is also able to disclose information about the sellers that the listing agent could not disclose without the seller's permission (for example, if a couple is getting a divorce and in a rush to close on the deal).

Oftentimes couples start the home-buying process by scouring newspaper ads and the Internet for homes they think they might like—then calling the agent listed in the ad. This is not the best way of going about the process. When you call the agent, you will likely be speaking to what's called the listing agent, who works for the seller. The listing agent's job is to keep the seller's best interests in mind and to try to get the seller the best possible price for his or her property. Agents are supposed to be impartial and able to represent both buyers and sellers on a given property. But many experts agree that it would be in the buyers' best interest to find their own agent first. Thus, when you're ready to buy, instead of scouring ads, first look for a real estate agent who will represent you. That person can then show you properties in line with your preferences and in your price range, including anything you might see in the newspaper.

You'll want to **pick the agent** you work with as **carefully** as you would a lawyer, accountant or other professional. Ask for recommendations from friends and relatives who have recently bought homes. If you call real estate companies to let them know you're in the market for a home, you'll want to interview—and meet with—prospective agents the same way you would any other expert before deciding to work with them.

Ask the following questions when having an initial phone conversation with a real estate agent:

- *Do you work full- or part-time?* This indicates how much time the agent may have to show you properties when it's most convenient for you, say at night and on the weekends. It also indicates how willing they may be to go the extra mile should problems arise. Finally, if they're only dabbling in real estate, there is a question of how up-to-date they keep on changes in the law and business practices.

- *For how long have you been selling homes?* Obviously, the more experienced the agent is, the better. When my husband and I sold our house, we ran into a problem with the buyers once we got to contract. The couple were suddenly on the outs— but that is not a legitimate reason to get out of a transaction given the stage we were at in the negotiation. Nonetheless, they started looking for things "wrong" with our house to try to cancel the deal. Our agent was not only highly experienced and savvy but worked hard with us and our lawyer to solve the problems that arose from the situation.

- *How well do you know the area in which you want to buy?* Sometimes agents only work in certain neighborhoods and don't know the surrounding areas. Ask where the broker has listings and make sure it encompasses every place you are considering. The agent should also have intimate knowledge of the community, the school system, etc. You're not just buying a house, you're buying into a neighborhood.

- *Are you also a mortgage broker?* This would give the agent more depth of experience in helping you to secure a loan. However, you should still shop around for a mortgage even if your agent is also a broker who can offer you terms on a deal.

- *Will you be working with us directly?* Sometimes very successful brokers pass clients off to an assistant once you've agreed to work with them.

You'll want to interview at least three agents in person. Explain what you are looking for and listen carefully to how the agent or Realtor proposes to help you find a home that will be just right for you. Before signing an agreement to work with an agent, first try to work with the person for a few days to see if they truly understand your wants and needs, and are responsive to your calls and to make sure it's a good personality fit. If that's not possible, see if you can sign an agreement that covers a few days, or try to work together, at least initially, on a nonexclusive basis. When you sign the agreement, be clear about the terms: If it only covers certain neighborhoods, how long it's in effect for and if there are any circumstances under which you are expected to pay the agent a commission. Typically the commission—6 percent is the average—is paid by the seller, and it is split between your agent and the listing agent. In addition, find out what happens if you buy a house that is sold by the owner—as in, who pays the agent's commission?

## Shopping for a Mortgage

You've found your dream house (yeah!), and you've put in an offer and it's been accepted (double yeah!). Now it's time to get financing. The type of loan you get will be based on the strength of your credit report and the amount you have to put down. Before you start making phone calls, educate yourself a bit about what the going interest rates are. You can check them out at HSH Associates (www.hsh.com), which tracks mortgage rates across the country.

Where should you shop for a mortgage? One good place to start is the **bank where you have your checking account**. Given that you are already a customer, perhaps you'll get a preferred rate. Check out your **credit union** if you belong to one, as well as local **savings and loans** (also called thrifts).

**Mortgage brokers** don't lend money; they find lenders for you (in other words, they broker a deal for you). When looking for a broker consider getting recommendations from friends or other professionals that you work with, such as your accountant. Mortgage brokers take your loan application and then shop it to a variety of banks, savings and loans and mortgage banks—at least that's how it's supposed to work. When a mortgage broker comes back to you with an offer, ask how many different lenders he or she got quotes from. You should also clarify how the broker is being paid. It could be by the lender, it could be by you (by way of points or an increased interest rate) or it could be both. If you are expected to provide some of the compensation, the amount is negotiable. Just be clear about how much the broker expects to be paid so you have a starting point for discussion.

Another loan source is a **mortgage banker**. An example of a mortgage banker is GMAC, which is owned by automaker GM. The mortgage banker takes your loan application and processes it. If you are approved and you accept the deal, it lends you the funds and services the loan (meaning it collects your monthly payment and pays your yearly taxes and homeowner's insurance, unless you opt to pay the latter two yourself).

When mortgage shopping, always mention that you are a first-time home buyer (and even if you're not, you may qualify as one if you haven't owned a home in three years). There may be special rates or programs for first-time buyers for which you qualify. In addition, there are state housing finance agencies that have special loan programs for low- to moderate-income buyers; they also offer favorable mortgage terms for those interested in rehabilitating urban areas. You do need to meet income requirements, and there is a cap on how much you can spend on a home, but it's worth checking out. You could be offered a fixed rate mortgage that is considerably lower than conventional loans with a low (3 percent) down payment requirement. To locate the housing agency in your state, go to the website for the National Council of State Housing Agencies (www.ncsha.org), then go to "About HFAs" and click on "State Housing Finance Agencies."

## Down Payment? What Down Payment?

Traditionally you would need at least a 20 percent down payment to get a loan, but there's a lot of creative financing today that means you could buy a house for less than 20 percent—or even no money—down. Here's how:

### Piggyback Loans

These loans can be structured in a variety of ways: 80/20, 80/15/5, 80/10/10. Let's say you don't have a down payment (or you want to use your cash for other things, like paying down credit card debt or student loans or investing). With an 80/20, you would take out two mortgages: One, the primary mortgage, finances 80 percent of loan, while the second, typically a line of credit with an adjustable rate, covers the 20 percent down payment. Structuring your financing this way helps you avoid paying Private Mortgage Insurance—always a good idea. The interest you would pay on the second mortgage tends to be less than what you would pay if you took a first loan covering more than 80 percent of the cost of the house and then paid Private Mortgage Insurance, says Diane Giarratano of NovaDebt. 80/15/5: Again, the primary mortgage finances 80 percent of the loan, the second mortgage or line of credit finances 15 percent (part of the down payment) and you pay the balance of the down payment in cash (5 percent). With an 80/10/10 you contribute a down payment of 10 percent.

If you don't have a 20 percent down payment, you might be eligible for a loan insured by the **Federal Housing Administration** (FHA). You need to have a solid credit history and sufficient income to pay the mortgage, but you can put down as little as 3 percent. Also, you can be approved with a higher debt-to-income ratio (up to 41 percent of gross income, including the mortgage payment). These loans do require you to carry Private Mortgage Insurance (figure that if your mortgage payment is $1,000, PMI would be around $100/month). There are limits on the amount you can borrow, set by the county you live in. These loans make it possible for low- to moderate-income borrowers who might not qualify for a conventional mortgage to buy a house.

The same can be said for a **VA loan**. When approaching lenders, be sure to let them know if you are a vet. You could qualify for a loan guaranteed by the Veteran's Administration. These loans require no down payment—the entire loan can be financed. Interest rates are competitive, and you're not required to carry PMI.

## Comparing Loans

You'll want to get between three and five offers—more than that and evaluating them could just become too confusing. Lenders are required to give you a good-faith estimate listing all fees due at closing. You should receive this statement within three days of your loan application. Review it carefully, comparing it to the estimates you get from other lenders.

Unfortunately, lenders don't exactly make it easy to compare offers since, for example, different lenders calculate APRs differently (the fees and costs they include can vary). In addition, if you're looking at a thirty-year fixed rate mortgage against one with an adjustable rate, you're not comparing apples to apples. Here is what you need to pay attention to and compare when considering loans:

*Interest rate:* Obviously the lower, the better.

*Length of the loan:* Fifteen, twenty, thirty years?

*Type of loan:* Does it have a fixed rate? (The interest rate remains the same throughout the life of the loan.) An ARM (Adjustable Rate Mortgage, meaning the interest rate fluctuates)? Or a combination of the two, called a hybrid loan (the initial interest rate is fixed for a set number of years, then it converts to an ARM)?

*Monthly mortgage payment:* What will it be? Be certain to find out if homeowner's insurance and taxes are included in the amount you're quoted. If not, the payment will be considerably higher.

*Annual Percentage Rate (APR):* The APR is the interest rate plus fees paid to get the loan. For example, it could include points, a loan processing fee, a document preparation fee and an underwriting fee, among others. This figure is important—it reflects how much you're paying just to get the financing—but it does not affect your monthly payment.

Here is how the APR might be advertised:

---

30-year fixed     5.62%     1 point     5.71% APR

---

The APR can be up to a quarter of a percent higher than the interest rate, so the higher the APR, the more expensive the loan. "This is where lenders make their money, in the points and various fees attached," notes Betty Messman, housing manager for Credit Counseling Service in Fort Worth. If the APR is considerably higher than the interest rate, you should question it: You're paying too much for the loan. Another way to suss out how much you're paying: Subtract out the fees not associated with the loan itself (ask the lender to help you identify these, if necessary), such as escrow fees, attorney fees, appraisal fees and title fees. Add up the remaining loan fees (points, origination fees, sales commissions) and you can see who is charging more. In particular, add up and compare the fees in Line 800s of the good-faith estimate, "Items Payable in Connection with the Loan." If there are any fees you don't understand, ask. And remember that many of these fees, particularly those in Lines 800–811, are negotiable.

> *Points:* An amount you pay to lower the interest rate. A point is equal to 1 percent of the loan amount. Example: One point on a $200,000 mortgage would be $2,000. If the loan doesn't include points, the interest rate will be higher than one that includes them. You'll need to carefully consider whether or not paying a point or two is worth it in the long run. No one wants to shell out more money than they have to when buying a house, but paying a couple thousand more upfront could save you thousands more if you're charged a higher interest rate. Note: You can pay for points with cash or finance them as part of the loan.

> *Private Mortgage Insurance (PMI):* This is insurance you are required to buy if you put less than 20 percent down on your home, or if you take out a government-insured FHA loan (which only requires a 3 percent down payment and sometimes less). The insurance does nothing to help or protect you—it protects the lender in case you default on the loan. Be sure to ask how much this adds to your monthly payment. You'll want to keep track as you build equity so that you can get this added expense dropped as soon as possible (once you've reached 20 percent equity).

> *Balloon payment:* At the end of the term of the loan, will the mortgage be paid off or will you owe a large lump sum? You'll likely want to avoid this.

*Prepayment penalty*: The lender charges you a fee if you sell or refinance your home, usually within a set period of time (typically two to five years from the start of the loan). This is fairly common with hybrid mortgages. Negotiate to get a mortgage without a prepayment penalty.

## Common Types of Mortgages

To reduce the amount you pay in interest as much as possible (barring accelerating payments!), the big picture idea is to try to match the loan to how long you'll be in the house.

### FIXED RATE

This is a very secure loan because the interest rate never changes. You know just what your monthly payments will be from now until you have your deed-burning party. This may be the mortgage to get if you plan on staying in the house for a long time (ten years or more) or if, when you're ready to trade up, you plan to keep your first home as an investment (e.g., rental property).

### ARM

An ARM, or Adjustable Rate Mortgage, comes with a fluctuating interest rate. The rate may rise after a set period of time, depending on market conditions (minimum and maximum rates are set as part of the deal). Thus, if interest rates increase so, too, would your monthly payment; if they decrease your monthly payment likewise should go down (but be sure to confirm that). If you do not plan on staying in your house for more than four or five years (typical for most couples), the ARM may be the option to go with—the interest rate you start out with is typically less than what you would be offered on a fixed rate mortgage.

## HYBRID

You start out with a fixed rate for a certain number of years, then it converts to an ARM. Couples with hybrid mortgages usually figure they'll sell before the fixed rate period is over.

## INTEREST-ONLY MORTGAGE

These types of loans have become popular in recent years. Here's how it works: You don't pay any amount toward the principal for the first, say, five years of the loan. (And you build no equity.) All you pay is the interest due. Therefore, you have a lower monthly payment. When the interest-only period is over, you start paying down the principal along with interest—only now you're in the position of having to pay it down in twenty-five instead of thirty years (on a thirty-year loan). You have to make up for lost time (the five years when you paid no principal) and your monthly payment increases substantially. Given this sudden increase, these loans aren't for everyone. Here are scenarios where an interest-only loan works best:

- You're a professional, say a doctor, who knows your salary will substantially increase over time. But for now you would rather have a lower monthly mortgage payment and put more money toward paying down your considerable education loans.

- You are wealthy and would rather take the money you would have put toward the principal each month and invest it where you could earn a potentially greater return.

- Your paycheck is irregular. This is typically the case with people who are self-employed. Perhaps your business is seasonal, or you just can't predict when you will win new contracts. In this case, the lower payments can help you make ends meet when money is tight. When you are flush, you can then accelerate the mortgage payments, *including* principal.

Unfortunately, interest-only loans are aggressively marketed to people who don't fall into one of the above categories. Brokers sometimes use the interest-only idea to get you into a bigger house than you could otherwise afford. (The monthly payment is initially lower, when you're paying only interest.) The expectation is that over time, your income will increase enough that you can afford the larger payments when they come due. There is also the expectation that the house will appreciate in value. You're not building equity in the house but you are expecting the market to do that for you.

It's a good theory, but there is no guarantee that things will work out once the interest-only period ends. The pitfalls lie in the fact that maybe your income will not have increased enough to manage the higher payments. Brokers will tell you that if that is the case, you could simply sell the house. But you don't know what future market conditions will be where you live either. There is a risk that the house won't have appreciated as much as you would need to make a profitable sale. You could end up owing more than the house is worth. Clearly the interest-only option carries with it some risk; if you don't fit one of the scenarios described above or if you tend to be more conservative in how you manage your money, it may not be for you.

## Closing the Deal

One day prior to closing, you should get from your mortgage lender or broker something called a HUD-1 Uniform Settlement Statement, a form required by the Department of Housing and Urban Development (HUD). The form lists all of the costs and credits (for example, if it's determined that the house needs a new roof and instead of having one installed, the seller gives you credit for the cost of one) you have coming to you at closing. Closing costs are typically between 1 and 3 percent of the value of the home, depending on the type of loan you get. (For example, on a $300,000 home, closing costs could range from $3,000 to $9,000.) There will be numerous fees that you should have already seen on the good faith estimate you got at the time of loan application. Examine the HUD-1 statement carefully. Check the math. Compare the figure on the HUD-1 to those on your good faith estimate. Pay special attention to "Items Payable in Connection with

## HOW TO TITLE YOUR HOUSE

The simplest way is to have it titled "Joint tenancy with right of survivorship" or "Tenancy by the entireties," as it's called in some states. In terms of estate planning, if something should happen to one of you the house won't go through the probate process and ownership automatically transfers to the surviving spouse. Owning the house together by "tenancy in common" means that you each own half (although you can divide it using any percentages you want). If something happens to you, your share is inherited by whomever you name in your will. If you don't have a will, the state determines how your property is divvied up—and your ownership share of the house may not go in its entirety to your spouse, as you may have wanted—another reason to have a will written. People with children from a previous marriage sometimes favor buying a home as tenants in common. Should the spouse with kids die, that share of the house could be willed to the children of the previous marriage. A final option is to hold the title in a living trust; your estate attorney can advise you if this is appropriate for your situation (see also chapter 12).

Loan," Lines 800s, and "Title Charges," Lines 1100s. If you see any fees or costs you don't understand (or which are suddenly showing up for the first time) be sure to question them before you get to closing the next day. For example, if you see a new line item of $400 for courier fees, that would certainly be something to inquire about.

There's a current trend where the seller helps pay some of the non-recurring (meaning one-time-only) closing costs. The reason a seller would agree to do this is because he or she knows the buyer may be cash-strapped at closing and it's a way to ensure a sale. Unless you're in a super-competitive market, it's worth asking your broker about this possibility when you first make the offer on the house.

## How to Buy a House in an Overheated Market

You're anxious to move into your own place, but the cost of housing is sky-high where you live. Short of winning the lottery, how can you make it happen? Consider buying with another party, who would become your coinvestor. For example, you might:

- Ask parents to help with the down payment. (But first see chapter 2, Sticky Money Situations.) Some parents are willing to help with the down payment as long as they eventually get it back, along with some of the house's appreciation. If a parent has $100,000 in a money market account earning 1 percent interest and could use some or all of it to help a child get into an investment appreciating at 6 or 10 percent a year, that's a good investment from the parents' perspective, notes money advisor Victoria Collins, CFP. One possible scenario is that after staying in the house for a few years, you and your DH sell it and repay the parents who provided the down payment, along with some of the profit (to be determined at the time of the loan). You then use the remainder of the profit to buy another house.

If you do this, be sure to put your agreement in writing to avoid any misunderstandings later.

- Buy a house with friends who are looking for an investment (as opposed to a place to live), then share the appreciation when you sell it. One possibility would be for you and your DH to live in the house and pay the mortgage, while maintenance expenses are shared with your coinvestors. Any such arrangement would require having a legal agreement drawn up outlining who is entitled to occupy the home, who pays for what and the percentage of profits you're each entitled to at the sale of the home, along with other terms as set out by your attorneys. It's not for everyone, but in some markets it may be one of the few ways to get into a house if you are in the middle-income range.

## Postpurchase Do's and Don'ts

You've just laid out quite a bit of cash for your fab new house. Yes, you want it to look great. You'll probably need some things like window treatments and a lawn mower. Still, this isn't the time to go nuts at Pottery Barn and Restoration Hardware, unless you have the cash to pay for your purchases. **Don't leap into credit card debt** once the card offers start flooding your mailbox.

After about six months, you'll start getting phone calls and letters saying now's a good time to refinance. But refinancing costs money. There are closing costs all over again, since the house needs to be appraised, there's another title search to confirm ownership of the property, there's another loan origination fee and perhaps points to pay the lender for preparing your loan, etc. **The rule of thumb is not to refinance until there are at least two percentage points' difference** in the interest rate you have and the one that's being offered. Even if that's the case, you still need to look at the bigger picture. It's important to consider how long it would take to recoup the closing costs. You'll want to live there long enough to enjoy the savings. Let's say that you lower your interest rate by a percentage point, and as a result, your mortgage payment is reduced by $100 per month. But your closing costs amount to $3,000. You would need to remain in your house for at least another 30 months ($3,000 divided by $100) to recoup those costs.

# 9. Saving for Retirement: Yes, You Need to Start Now

### Make This Your Mantra: Don't Use Retirement Savings for Anything but Retirement!

Julie, thirty-four, is a Milwaukee-based publications secretary who is just finishing her college education. Her husband, John, thirty-five, is a store manager. After almost a year of marriage, she says they don't talk much about retirement savings, even though, Julie says, "I know we should." She doesn't know how much is in John's IRA, and she herself only has $4,000 set aside. "I've got huge student loans," she notes. "We're talking in the neighborhood of $40,000 or $50,000." Julie says John isn't currently adding to his IRA. "We're focused on getting a house," she says.

Retirement seems like a long ways off, doesn't it? It's probably one of the last things on your mind, right? It's understandable if, like Julie and John, you feel hard-pressed to save for the future. But given the realities your generation and those that follow will face, it is absolutely crucial that you start saving for retirement, even if it's only $100 per month. Or $50 per month to start. Something!

Here's why the urgency: Traditionally, people financed retirement using the old "three-legged stool" approach. One leg was a *pension* that was paid for by their company. You may say, a pension, what's that? Correct response, since it is highly unlikely that you will get one. A company-paid pension meant that when you retired, your former company (that you worked for for, like, twenty or thirty years) rewarded your loyalty and hard work by paying you a monthly retirement benefit from the day you retired until the day you died. The bigger your salary while working, the bigger your pension. Cool, right?

These days, pensions have gone the way of electric typewriters. They are quite hard to find. In order to get one, first, you would need to work at a major corporation (or, perhaps, be a member of a union) where you are most likely to be offered a pension. Second, even if you are working at a major corporation right now, what are the chances that you will spend your entire career there, making it possible for you to earn a fat pension? Get my drift? Finally, let's say you do work at a major corporation *and* you stay there your entire career. There is *still* a chance that your company could fall on hard times or go through belt-tightening or even file for bankruptcy and reduce or eliminate the pension. This is happening right now (think Polaroid and USAirways), where people who *did* stay at a company long enough to earn a pension are finding the rug pulled out from under them. Some company pensions are insured (because the company pays for the insurance) by the Federal Pension Benefit Guaranty Corporation, a government agency that takes over failed pension funds. In those cases, the employee would still get a pension, but the amount of the benefit would be cut dramatically. So Mr. Well-Paid Exec who thought he was cruising by on a pension of $100,000 a year is now getting, like $22,000. (Oh, yeah, and traditionally men are more likely than women to have pensions.) Okay, so scratch the pension, not that you were counting on it anyway. If you get one, consider it gravy.

## Social Security

Social Security traditionally was considered leg #2 in the three-legged stool. You've probably heard a lot about how Social Security is going to run out of money because of all the baby boomers who will suck money out of the system, without enough workers coming behind them to pay in and keep it afloat. (Social Security is a pay-as-you-go system.) Social Security may not run out of money altogether, but if you want to make sure it is well-funded for your retirement, you and all of your friends should have sixteen kids each, ensuring more workers to pay into the system. Okay, that may not be the most practical answer. But you need to be aware that your benefits may be cut. (Read: *You* have to save more!) Here it is, straight from the mouth of the agency (you can check out its website at www.socialsecurity.gov): "Unless changes are made, when you (twenty-five-year-old) reach age sixty-three in 2042, benefits for all retirees could be cut by 27 percent and could continue to be reduced every year thereafter. If you live to be 100 years old in 2079 (which will be more common by then), your scheduled benefits could be reduced by 33 percent from today's scheduled levels." On that happy note, we refer to the third leg of the stool, which is . . .

## Your Savings

Given that we just kicked two legs out from under the three-legged stool, it should become all too chillingly clear that what's primarily left for your retirement is what you and your DH manage to save. This is a very serious issue. Even though you probably don't want to think about it now—I know, you're just starting your married life together!—the truth is that you *have* to think about it now. Unfortunately, it is not optional. If you want to have adequate money in retirement, to live the kind of life you want to live and to do the kinds of things you'll want to do (like, quit working, travel, etc.), retirement savings absolutely must be a nonnegotiable line item on your budget. Why? Because the one thing you have in your favor—time—is the thing you need to take advantage of now, while you can.

In chapter 7, we talked about compound interest and how invested money grows. If you start early enough, you'll have much more money in your till than if you start late. Let's say that at age twenty-six, you begin to save a modest $3,000/year ($250/month) in a traditional IRA, and you earn an 8 percent rate of return. By age sixty-seven, you would have nearly $1 million—$948,300. Let's say, on the other hand, you decide to delay. You don't start your $3,000 annual savings plan until you hit age forty, but you still earn 8 percent. At age sixty-seven you'd only have $285,300. In both of those examples, the money is pretax, so you'd have even less to spend after Uncle Sam takes his cut.

## How Much Should You Save?

Kathleen and Ty could be the poster couple for saving. Kathleen, thirty, is an account administrator, while Ty, thirty-four, is a project manager. The Irvine, California, couple's household income is a healthy $150,000, making it possible for them to sock money away for the future. To their credit, that's exactly what they're doing. They each put aside 15 percent of their salaries into 401(k)s at work, and IRAs. The couple have $92,000 in their retirement nest egg thus far; the money is invested in aggressive stock funds. Kathleen's main worry is that, given the unpredictability of the market, "the funds we've selected won't perform as we hope they will."

So, how much should you be putting aside? The traditional wisdom has been that you would need about 70 percent of your final year's salary as income in the first year of retirement (and multiply that by the number of years you expect to live to get a total. Experts say that given medical advances, you should figure you'll live to be 100). This figure assumes your mortgage payments are reduced or eliminated, that you're no longer paying for things like kids' college and that you're no longer saving for retirement—you're living off your savings/earnings and whatever you get from Social Security. So if any of those things are not true, you'll need more.

Clearly, it's difficult to put an exact figure on how much to save, since there are so many unknowns in your life at this point. Really, how do you know what your salary will be in thirty years (by one standard you could figure your salary will compound at 6 percent a year) or how much your stock investments will earn (the experts are estimating 8 percent over the next decade, down from the historic 10 to 11 percent), or how much health insurance and out-of-pocket medical expenses will actually cost. (The bad news is that out-of-pocket spending on health-care costs will only increase, with expectations that it will eat up nearly 30 percent of after-tax income by 2030.) Even today retirees are finding their employer-paid health insurance vanishing into thin air. According to Employee Benefit Research Institute (EBRI), only about 15 percent of workers can expect to receive this benefit thirty years hence.

Enough said. You know you're going to need a major chunk of cash. How to get there? Financial experts agree that a minimum amount for you and your DH to save in a retirement savings account would be **10 percent to 15 percent of your gross (pretax) salary each year**. So let's say you earn $50,000 and your DH earns $75,000. You would then be setting aside $416 per month and he would be saving $625 per month in a qualified savings plan. You may be thinking, *Are you nuts?!* Hey, I didn't write the rules. I'm just telling you what you have to do if you don't want to wake up hysterical at forty-five or fifty years old, realizing you have nothing in the bank. Even if you can't put aside 10 percent or 15 percent right now, start small. Try putting 2 percent into your 401(k), then slowly build to 3 percent or 4 percent. That's a better strategy than thinking, "I can't do the full amount so I won't do anything." Systematically saving produces successful results, even if you begin with modest amounts. Automatic withdrawals from your paycheck, regardless of what the market is doing, are key. And here's a thought: Each time you get a raise, quickly—that is, rush!—contact your HR department or plan administrator and increase the percentage going into your 401(k) plan. That way, you won't miss that part of your raise because you'll never have seen it. If you invest in IRAs, set up automatic withdrawals from your checking account.

If you would like to get a more precise fix on how much to save, check out one of the calculators at www.choosetosave.org. I can't stress enough how important it is for *both* you and your DH to put away money for retirement, starting now, since it'll take both of your efforts to reach your goal (which, don't laugh, could easily be $1 million for the two of you). In addition (not to be pessimistic, just covering all the bases), in the event that you divorce, there will be a more sizeable nest egg to split if you are both socking money away.

## You and Your 401(k)/403(b)/457 Plan

In the old days, workers had access to something called defined benefit plans. The company invested money on your behalf, then rewarded you with a pension when you retired. If your company offered such a plan, you usually had to stay at the company a minimum number of years—say, five—to become eligible for the pension. The amount you received was determined by your salary and longevity at the company.

These days, you are more likely to be offered a defined contribution plan (meaning you get to contribute) called the 401(k), after the part of the tax code that covers it (403[b] for nonprofits and 457 for government workers). Your contributions are made on a pretax basis, cutting your current tax bill. The idea is that you'll be taxed for the contributions and earnings when you tap into the money at retirement age (and at that point you may be in a lower tax bracket, so you'll pay less in taxes). Often a company will match a certain percentage of your contribution (typically 50 cents for every $1 you put in), up to a percentage of your salary, typically 6 percent, which would result in a 3 percent match. Some companies pay out the match with company stock, although some will then allow you to diversify and put it into other investing options within the plan. The government determines the rules, including how much you are allowed to sock away in your 401(k) each year. In 2005, employees can contribute a maximum of $14,000 of their pay; that will rise to $15,000 in 2006. Note: You may not be able to contribute the full amount if you earn more than $90,000. Check with your plan's administrator for details. The reason is so that highly compensated employees don't benefit disproportionately over their less well-paid colleagues.

What are current 401(k) plan trends, and might you be a part of them? A 2003 survey of 2.5 million employees by Hewitt Associates, a human resources outsourcing and consulting firm in Lincolnshire, Illinois, found the following:

- *Not enough of you participate.* Seventy-six percent of eligible employees contribute to their 401(k), but only 45.4 percent of workers ages twenty to twenty-nine were socking money into their plan. (Please don't take that as a reason to justify why you don't contribute if you aren't yet doing so.)

---

### GO FIGURE!

If you would like to guesstimate what your 401(k) will be worth in the future, there is a handy calculator at www.quicken.com (click on Investing).

---

- *You need to save more.* The average contribution rate was 8.1 percent, but nearly one-third of participants age twenty to twenty-nine contributed under 5 percent of pay. Friendly reminder: The amount to work toward is 10 percent to 15 percent of your annual pay.

- *There's a lack of proper diversification.* About one-third of participants select just one or two investment options within the plan. If that describes you, please go back to chapter 7 and read the section on diversification and asset allocation. On average, plans surveyed offer fourteen investment options, including everything you need to properly diversify: Equity funds (large-, mid- or small-cap funds or an index fund, with a large-cap fund being most common), balanced funds, bond funds, money market funds, stable value funds (which invest in bonds and interest-bearing contracts) and foreign equity funds.

- *You're holding too much company stock.* 26.8 percent invest half or more of their plan balances in company stock; the average balance in company stock is 40.5 percent. Remember Enron and WorldCom? To be properly diversified, experts recommend that you invest no more than 20 percent of your money in company stock.

- *Lifestyle funds may be misunderstood.* These funds, offered by 38 percent of the plans surveyed, contain a diversified, premixed portfolio. A lifestyle fund (also called an asset allocation fund) can be a good choice if you don't have the time or inclination to research the funds offered, make your own selections and manage your portfolio. However, only 13.2 percent of 401(k) participants put all of their noncompany stock balance into the lifestyle fund, suggesting they are not aware that the fund is already diversified. Sometimes plan participants select more than one lifestyle fund, which can result in overdiversification and mediocre earnings.

It's worth noting that if you have access to a 401(k) at work with a company match and you're not contributing, you're doing yourself even more of a disservice because you're leaving money on the table. When your company offers a match, it's saying that it's willing to help you save: Let it! One survey of 130,000 employees by Aon Consulting found that those who turned down the match in 2003 missed out on a total of $89 million in employer contributions. That's one "trend" you want to miss out on.

## What If There's No Company Match?

Research shows that a company match is a powerful motivator for employees to fund their 401(k) plans. But these days, some companies—even large ones, such as Ford Motor and Charles Schwab—have suspended or eliminated the match, looking to trim costs.

One powerful reason to contribute to your company 401(k), even if there is no match, is that the upper limits for saving are greater than that of an IRA. In 2005, you can sock $14,000 into tax-deferred 401(k) versus $4,000 in an IRA. But suppose you're not saving over $4,000 a year? What should you do? First check out the investment options in your company's 401(k) plan. If there's a strong selection of mutual funds to choose from (meaning you've logged onto Morningstar, looked at how many stars each fund in the mix has earned, checked out the performance record and expenses, etc., as described in chapter 7), you may want to go ahead and invest in the 401(k), even if there is no match. At least you know you can increase your savings if you want to, and who knows, maybe your company will introduce a match in the future. Otherwise put your savings into an IRA in the mutual funds of your choice.

## What Is Holding You Back?

Danielle and Oren are more concerned about short-term goals of paying off her student loans ($26,000) and saving for a house than retirement savings. It's understandable. The couple are concerned about where they're going to buy once they're ready, given the high cost of home ownership in the New York metropolitan area, where they live. In terms of retirement savings, she has an IRA with $3,000 and he has a 401(k), though Danielle is uncertain of the balance and doesn't think Oren is currently adding to it. She adds that Oren's parents, who are deceased, left him a house in Israel, which he rents. "He thinks of that as retirement money," she says.

Like this couple, you may feel the weight of today's financial priorities, such as buying a house and paying off debt. In their case, it's certainly a plus that they have a rental property that will throw off income, but they realize they will need to do more.

Let's examine why you may not be contributing (and hopefully shoot some of those excuses down). Perhaps you don't want to put money in the plan because you have debt. That may or may not be a wise decision. If you have credit card debt at high interest rates (18 percent or more), you're right to focus on paying that down, even if it means sacrificing contributing to a 401(k). But how about seeing if you could move those balances to a card with a lower interest rate, and you'll pay the balance down faster. As soon as you pay off your credit cards, channel the money you used to send the card companies to your 401(k). Student loans, on the other hand, shouldn't prevent you from making contributions. What I mean by that is you wouldn't want to step up paying back your student loan over paying into the 401(k). The tax savings realized from the 401(k) contributions will outdo the low interest you're paying on your education loans.

On the other hand, perhaps you're focused on saving for a house—a worthy goal, since home ownership is certainly one component of a healthy retirement plan. If you can only seriously save for one goal (meaning, the house down payment), at least put a small amount into the 401(k) so that you're in the habit of investing (and to get as much of any match offered as possible). Once you have the down payment, ramp up your 401(k) contribution.

What about borrowing from your plan for the house down payment? If your 401(k) plan allows it, and most do, you could borrow half of your balance, up to $50,000, to put toward a house down payment. But it's not the best source of funds. If you changed jobs or got

---

## STASH IT, DON'T CASH IT!

You and your DH may change jobs a few times throughout your twenties and thirties. Great, nothing wrong with moving on and moving up. One glitch, however: Research shows that when employees have less than $20,000 in their retirement savings account, 85 percent take the money and spend it. Bad move. The balance may be on the low side, but you'll take away the effect of compound interest if you raid your retirement fund. It's the time value of money that gets you to the place you want to be, not the amount you put in. Indeed, you stand to lose a lot since you'll have to pay taxes on the money you withdraw, plus a 10 percent early withdrawal penalty. Let's say you're in the 25 percent tax bracket and cash out $15,000 in your 401(k). All you'll come away with is $9,750, with $5,250 going to Uncle Sam. The smart move? Roll the money over into an IRA, or into your new employer's plan. Sure, you could leave the money in your old employer's plan, but you can keep a better eye on it (you'll no longer hear the scuttlebutt on how your old company is faring) if you take it with you and roll it over into a new tax-advantaged account.

---

laid off, the loan would likely be due in full within a short period of time. (According to a Hewitt Associates survey of 489 companies, 29 percent of the plans surveyed allow former employees to continue making loan payments.) Still, if immediate repayment is expected and you couldn't come up with the cash, you'd have to pay taxes and a 10 percent penalty on the outstanding balance.

## Coordinating Retirement Savings

Beth, thirty-two, a writer, and Steven, thirty-eight, a filmmaker and teacher, are a New York City couple who, like many other newlyweds, are focused on a house purchase, which they expect to make in five years. Still, they are making some inroads into their retirement savings. "Every year my accountant suggests I add to my IRA, which has very little money in it. This is the first year I was able to do it," says Beth. She points out that Steven is contributing a healthy 10 percent of his salary to a retirement plan at work, where he earns a company match.

Lisa, thirty-four, who works in customer service for a utility in Lewiston, Idaho, and John, forty-five, a recovery boiler operator, are each saving 10 percent of their salaries in their respective 401(k) plans, plus a Roth IRA for Lisa. With a household income of $75,000, they've made retirement savings a priority. "I'm always concerned about the uncertainty of Social Security," says Lisa. Before the couple married in 2004, they each owned their own home. "We've turned mine into a rental, which will eventually be retirement income for us," Lisa adds.

Naturally, everyone's circumstances are different, but these couples are proactively working toward their retirement nest eggs. But they may be more of an exception than the rule. After talking to many brides and financial planners, it's more common for couples not to have retirement savings on the radar screen, much less coordination of retirement plans. "They're lucky if they know what the other has in his or her 401(k) or IRA," notes Greg McGraime, a certified financial planner and vice president at JPMorgan Chase Bank in New York City.

You're now saving for a joint goal (even though you maintain separate accounts), so it's important to discuss your progress in working toward it. Certainly you can maintain a sense of autonomy and make your own fund selections, based on the amount of risk with which you are comfortable. But it's good to have a general discussion about how you're each invested. Otherwise, you could end up duplicating efforts, or you may not be diversified enough. For example, together you could be taking on too much or too little risk for your portfolio. If you're in all tech and so is your DH—your entire nest egg could be tied up in one industry. Ideally the two of you should sit down together to review your portfolios to make sure you have a good total mix, and to make sure you're on track for reaching your joint goal. Here's how:

1. First compare how much you each are saving for retirement (percent of salary) and where the money is being saved (e.g., in an IRA or 401[k]).

2. If it's in a 401(k), is there a company match? If so, are you each putting in as much as possible to get the maximum match? If not, discuss when you might be able to boost your savings.

3. Review how long you each must remain on the job to be vested and receive the company match. If possible, you'll want to stay on the job long enough to collect those funds.

4. Get out your most recent statements for any 401(k)s and/or IRAs and review balances. If you did a rough estimate of how much you'll need in your retirement nest egg, are you on track for reaching that goal?

5. Review your asset allocation, making sure you each have a combination of stocks, bonds and cash. If one of you wants to

invest more conservatively than the other, fine, but if you are too conservative you won't end up with as big a nest egg as you otherwise could. As you reach middle age, that's when you can start to alter your asset allocations so that you're less heavily in stocks (about 50 percent, as opposed to 70 percent or 80 percent now) and more in bonds, which are less risky.

6. Review if either of you has access to a company-paid pension. If so, determine when you or he will be vested in it (how many years must you remain on the job). Talk to HR to get a rough estimate of what you can expect to receive; this figure should also be factored into your planning. If you know you have X dollars coming from a pension, you may need to save that much less.

7. Be sure to review your investments once a year and rebalance your portfolios as necessary (see chapter 7 on rebalancing). In addition, you'll want to review how much you're each saving and increase it with each successive raise, until you get to that magical 10 percent to 15 percent of gross pay.

If one or both of you don't have access to a 401(k), what then? You can each still save—in an IRA.

## IRA Options

You're undoubtedly familiar with IRAs—short for Individual Retirement Account. Perhaps you already have one. If not, here's a brief rundown of the various types available. If you do not have access to a retirement savings plan at work, you would be well advised to start saving each year in an IRA. You can open one with any brokerage firm, bank, credit union or mutual fund company.

# Traditional IRA

In 2005 the limit on IRA contributions is $4,000, which may be fully or partially tax deductible, or not deductible at all. The limit remains $4,000 through 2007, then goes up to $5,000 in 2008. Here is what determines whether or not you can deduct your contribution to a traditional IRA:

- your income

- your filing status (if you file married jointly or married filing separately)

- whether or not you are also covered by a retirement plan at work

What follows is a breakdown of the rules (as they apply to married couples), which determine whether or not you can deduct your contribution. Bear in mind that the income limits and amount you can contribute tend to change each year or so. Before making any decisions, be sure to check with the IRS (www.irs.gov, publication 590) or your accountant to be certain you have the most recent information.

## YOU ARE COVERED BY A RETIREMENT PLAN AT WORK

"Covered" means not only that you are offered a retirement plan, but that you are participating in it. Let's say that you are. If you file a joint return, you can take a full deduction of your IRA contribution if your modified adjusted gross income (AGI) is $65,000 or less. If your modified AGI is more than $65,000 but less than $75,000, you get a partial deduction. If your AGI is greater than $75,000, sorry, no deduction for you. You can still save in an IRA (and your money grows on a tax-deferred basis), you just can't deduct your contribution on your tax return.

177

What if you file married, filing separately? You can take a partial deduction if your modified AGI is less than $10,000. Anything over that? Forget it.

Important note: You'll want to make sure that your employer accurately reports to the IRS whether or not you are covered by a retirement plan. Why? Because if you are *not* covered, and you invest in an IRA, taking the deduction, you could get hit with an excise penalty by the IRS if it is inaccurately reported that you are covered. How do you check to be sure your status has been accurately reported? Check your W-2, specifically box 13. If you are not covered, that box should *not* be checked. If it is, return it to HR for correction. According to an IRS spokesperson, this is a common mistake (checking the box when it shouldn't be), since many companies outsource their payroll activities.

## YOU ARE *NOT* COVERED BY A RETIREMENT PLAN AT WORK

If you file a joint return, and your spouse also is *not* covered by a retirement plan at work, you can make any amount of money and your contribution is fully deductible. What if you file a joint return and your spouse *is* covered by a retirement plan at work? If your modified AGI is $150,000 or less, you can fully deduct your contribution. If you make more than $150,000 but less than $160,000, you get a partial deduction. If your AGI is over $160,000, forget it: no deduction for you.

What if you file married, filing separately? If your spouse also is *not* covered by a retirement plan at work, you can make any amount of money and you can deduct the full amount of your contribution. Suppose your spouse *is* covered by a plan at work? You only get a partial deduction if your modified AGI is less than $10,000.

## FIGURING OUT THE PARTIAL DEDUCTION

I hate to be repetitive, but I must again refer you to IRS Publication 590, which has a handy worksheet for figuring out the deduction. If you are flummoxed, call your accountant or the IRS directly at 1-800-829-1040. They have great customer service and are quite clear in answering questions.

## Roth IRA

With the Roth, you can't deduct the amount you contribute, but you don't pay tax on the earnings when you take the money out in retirement. That's huge. Again, in 2005 you can contribute $4,000 to a Roth. You have to have earned income, and you can't put in more than you've earned. This is a moot point if you have a full-time job. But if you don't and you've earned, say, $2,000 for the year, you couldn't put in more than that amount.

There are income restrictions for the Roth. You need to meet these conditions to contribute:

- Your modified AGI is less than $150,000 and you file jointly. In that case, each of you can open a Roth and fund it to the tune of $4,000. If your AGI is at least $150,000 but less than $160,000, the amount you can contribute is reduced. If your AGI is $160,000 or more, you cannot contribute to a Roth IRA.

- Your AGI is more than zero but less than $10,000, you lived with your spouse at some point during the year and file married, separate. Under that scenario you can contribute a reduced amount; otherwise, no Roth IRA for you. Perhaps one compelling reason to consider filing a married joint return.

- As long as you meet the income requirements, you can contribute to a Roth even if you have a traditional IRA and a

401(k). However, you each only get one annual $4,000 contribution. So, for example, if you only put $2,000 into a traditional IRA, you could then only put $2,000 into a Roth. Your spouse can do the same.

---

## SCORECARD: ROTH VS TRADITIONAL IRA

What's so attractive about the Roth? Let's take a look.

| ROTH | TRADITIONAL IRA |
| --- | --- |
| Contributions are not tax-deductible | Contributions may be tax-deductible |
| Contributions can be withdrawn at any time (they were made with after-tax dollars) | Tax-deductible contributions withdrawn before age 59½ will incur taxes and a 10% penalty |
| Earnings are tax-free* | Earnings are taxed |
| Can add to it forever | No contributions can be made after age 70½ |
| Can leave money invested forever | Must start taking distributions at age 70½ |

*Assuming withdrawals are made after you reach age 59½ and the account has been open for at least five years.*

Note: Early withdrawals (pre age 59½) from traditional IRAs are taxed, but are not subject to the 10% penalty if the funds are needed in the case of disability, death of the IRA holder or if the funds are used to pay for higher education or to buy a first home ($10,000 limit). For Roth IRA investors, a distribution can be made tax-free before the age of 59½ if the account has been open for at least five years and if the reason is death of the Roth IRA owner, disability or the purchase of a first home ($10,000 lifetime limitation).

---

## Saving for the Self-Employed

If you're making your own way in the work world, you're far from alone. According to the Bureau of Labor Statistics, 18.2 percent of twenty- to thirty-four-year-olds are their own bosses (with unincorporated businesses). If you're in the ranks of the self-employed, you'll need to create your own retirement benefits plan. Here are the options:

## SEP IRA (Simplified Employee Pension)

It's easy to set up; just fill out IRS form 5305-SEP (available at www.irs.gov). Your savings go into a traditional IRA, but the rules for how much you can contribute are different, since it's a SEP. You'll need to do a calculation to figure out the most you can put in each year, but generally speaking it can be up to 25 percent of self-employment income with a maximum of $41,000 in 2005, whichever is less. To complete this calculation, there is a worksheet in IRS Publication 560

---

### A NEAT IRA TRICK

Suppose you have a big bill to pay—and you don't have the funds now, but you will in a month or two. What to do? You can take a tax-free, penalty-free withdrawal from your IRA, *as long as you repay the money within sixty days*. I used this strategy once to tide us over in a pinch when we were selling our house. If you do it, you *must* make sure you repay the money to your account within sixty days, or Uncle Sam will hit you with a 10 percent penalty *and* you'll have to pay taxes on the withdrawal. You can take this mini-loan once every twelve months.

---

(Retirement Plans for Small Business), or have your accountant do it for you.

## SIMPLE IRA (Savings Incentive Match Plan for Employees of Small Employers)

This is an option for small business owners, but individuals who work for themselves can take advantage of it as well. To set one up, complete Form 5304-SIMPLE. In 2005 you can defer up to $10,000 of earned income into the plan. You would select a SEP IRA if the amount you could afford to contribute is greater than that available in the SIMPLE IRA. If you have questions about either, check with your accountant, or send an e-mail to RetirementPlanQuestions@irs.gov (include your phone number) or call the IRS at 1-877-829-5500 between 8 A.M. and 6:30 P.M., EST.

## KEOGH

Such plans are more complicated to set up than the SIMPLE IRA and SEP IRA. It'll require the help of an accountant, but the limits of what you can save (and deduct from your taxes) are greater, up to $41,000 per year in 2005 or 100 percent of your salary, whichever is less, depending on the type of plan you select.

## Just Do It!

Gosh, couldn't we all use a few extra bucks every paycheck to 1) put toward the mortgage or a house down payment 2) pay the bills 3) put something away for a rainy day 4) go out to dinner etc.? The fact is, the majority of us are faced with making trade-offs in how we spend our money. We all have limits, unless you happen to be billionaire George Soros or Warren Buffett. And even they have to decide the best use for their funds . . . they just have more to spread around!

As you and your DH live your lives, many more needs will be vying for your attention and for the cash in your wallets. Just wait until you have kids! Still, it's important not to ever let retirement saving fall by the wayside. If you're already stashing away some cash, good for you. But if not, make a promise to yourself to start saving as soon as possible (even if it means cutting back on discretionary spending) and keep it. You deserve to have the resources you need not only now, but in the future. You can make it happen!

# 10. Insurance: Health, Car, Home/Renters, Disability and Life

Once you marry, it's a good idea to review all of your existing insurance policies, alongside those of your DH. First you're checking to make sure the amount of coverage you have is still appropriate and adequate, and second, you're figuring out where there are any gaps in coverage. You'll also want to review how much you're paying for existing policies. You may find that you'll save money by moving your policies with one insurer, where it is feasible to do so.

## Health Insurance

Should you maintain your individual policies or should one of you join the other's plan? Here are the key factors to consider:

1. *How much will it cost out of pocket if you each stay on your own plans? How much will it cost if you go on his plan, or if he goes on yours?* Ask your HR department to give you a breakdown of

how much more you would pay each month to cover your spouse. Also compare your plans in terms of the cost of individual deductibles, the copay for doctor's visits, the cost of seeing doctors outside your plan and prescription coverage.

2. *Consider the scope of coverage offered.* Maybe your DH has a great plan covering everything—medical, dental, vision—and you have a crappy plan by comparison. It could be worth it to pay extra to join his group.

3. *If you are wedded to certain doctors, make sure they participate in the plan you're considering.* For some people, this could be the make or break in deciding on a plan.

4. *Take into account who has the steadier job.* If, for example, your DH hears rumblings about outsourcing, don't hop onto his plan until things settle down.

5. *If one or both of you have a cafeteria benefits plan that allows you to pick and choose your benefits, review the offerings.* For example, you might want to go on your DH's health plan so that you could pick up disability coverage from your employer.

If, after comparing the two plans, you're thinking of joining your DH's or vice versa, what about preexisting conditions? And what the heck is a preexisting condition anyway? "It is a condition you have received treatment for, diagnosis of, or consulted with a licensed doctor over within x months of your new health insurance contract," says Brian Ash, chairman-elect with the Life and Health Insurance Foundation for Education. "It might also extend to include symptoms of an ailment for which a reasonable person would have sought medical attention but didn't." By law, a preexisting condition should be covered without a waiting period if you have had health insurance during the previous twelve months. If you haven't had health coverage, preexisting conditions could be excluded for a waiting period of up to twelve months, depending on how long you were without insurance. **Under group policies, pregnancy is not considered a preexisting condition. But if you buy an individual policy, pregnancy is considered a preexisting condition.** This provides yet another reason why it's important not to let your health insurance lapse.

## If You and Your DH Don't Have Health Insurance

According to the National Survey of Families most recent survey, young adults between the ages of nineteen and thirty-four are at greater risk of being without health insurance for twelve months or longer than any other age group. If you and your DH fall into this group, you're in the company of some 45 million Americans (of all ages) who are flying without a health insurance net. Perhaps you work for a small company that doesn't provide coverage, or you're between jobs, or you're self-employed. Whatever the cause, that's a scary place to be. You may be healthy, but things can happen . . . a car accident, a cycling mishap . . . not to mention, what if you get pregnant? A hospitalization could set you back many thousands of dollars. One sobering thought: Sky-high medical bills are one of the top reasons people end up in bankruptcy. To protect your health and your finances it would be best for you to find coverage and to lay out for the monthly premiums—there are affordable plans to be found, but how affordable depends a lot on where you live. Services, including health care, tend to cost more in large, metropolitan areas.

Here are a few possible sources:

- Join a trade or professional association that offers health insurance. Belonging to a group plan costs less than buying an individual policy. For example, as a writer I could buy a policy from the Author's Guild, or from a group for media professionals called Media Bistro. Both are located in New York City.

- Sometimes regional plans are available. To find one, do a Google search such as, "health insurance in _____" (name of your state or city). In New York City and the surrounding counties, for example, a group called Working Today offers health insurance to independent workers who are employed at least part-time in the following fields: nonprofit, media, technology, financial services and child care. State insurance, though pricey, is available for people who have been turned down everywhere else; it covers people with serious medical conditions.

- See if your college's alumni association offers health insurance. Or check to see if a social or civic group to which you belong makes insurance available to members.

- Ask another professional, such as your doctor or accountant, if they know of any good plans serving your area.

- For an individual policy, talk to an insurance broker. You might also check out www.ehealthinsurance.com. You may be able to find something affordable that would at least give you coverage for basic office visits and hospitalization.

## Quick Health Insurance Review

If you need to buy a policy, what should you be looking for? First, if you are between jobs or are waiting for coverage at a new job to kick in, look into buying a short-term policy covering between two and six months. (This is assuming you or your DH didn't leave, voluntarily or otherwise, a job that offered health insurance. If you did, you are entitled to buy health insurance under your former group's plan for up to eighteen months under a federal law known as COBRA—Consolidated

Omnibus Budget Reconciliation Act of 1985. By law, you would be required to pay 102 percent of the premium charged to your employer. Ask your plan's administrator for details.) But let's say you don't have access to COBRA. Next you need to decide which type of policy you want. Here are the possibilities:

## MANAGED CARE

You've likely been covered under this type of plan in the past. Managed Care comes in three flavors: Health Maintenance Organizations (HMO), Preferred Provider Organizations (PPO) and Point-of-Service (POS) plans. With managed care, the insurer has arrangements with certain doctors, hospitals and health-care providers to provide various services at reduced cost. Doctors agree to this arrangement since membership in the plans drives patients to their offices. There are some differences between the policies.

*HMO.* You have a primary care physician whom you've selected from the plan, sort of the "gatekeeper" to your health care. You have to see this doctor and get a referral before going to a specialist. You may need to pay a copay of $10 or so for office visits. If you're going with an HMO, financially it makes sense to use their network of doctors. If you go out-of-network, you pay the bill.

*PPO.* This plan is slightly less restrictive than an HMO. You go to a doctor within the network and pay a copay for office visits. You can select your own specialist from within the network, and you don't have to see your primary care physician first before trotting off to the allergist, etc. If you go out of network you have to meet a deductible before receiving reimbursement. Then you would pay coinsurance (at a higher rate than if you were in-network). You would also pay the difference between what the doctor charges and what the plan is willing to pay.

This difference would also be greater because the doctor, not having an arrangement with the PPO, would charge you more for services.

*POS.* This is an HMO with a twist. Your primary care doctor would typically refer you to specialists within the plan. But if they refer you to someone outside of it, the office visit or treatment would still be covered.

You may be wondering, How will my DH and I pay for this? Well, this is why people look for jobs offering health insurance—the employer pays a good chunk of the premium (although many employers have been asking employees to ante up more out of their own pockets in recent years, due to rising insurance costs). Still, if employer-paid health insurance isn't on the horizon, all is not lost. If you opt for a large deductible on your plan, you could get some tax relief through a health savings account.

## HEALTH SAVINGS ACCOUNTS (HSA)

If you are covered by a qualified High Deductible Health Plan (HDHP)—you could benefit from an HSA: They allow you to sock away money on a pretax basis for paying your medical bills. That means you can deduct the amount you've put into one of these accounts on your tax return, lowering the amount of income that is taxed. The money is invested and grows tax-free. When you withdraw funds to pay medical expenses, the earnings are not taxed. (The concept is similar to that of an IRA.) In order to qualify, you have to have medical coverage with an annual deductible of at least $1,000 (if the policy is for you only) or $2,000 (for family coverage). In addition, the plan must have in place a limit on the amount you pay each year for out-of-pocket medical expenses (including deductibles and copays). The limits are $5,000 for a policy covering one person or $10,000 for a family plan.

There are also limits on how much you can add to an HSA each year. It's the lesser of your policy deductible, or $2,600 if the policy is just for you, or $5,150 for a family plan. If, for example, the deductible on your solo health insurance policy was $1,000, that is the amount you could put in. If the deductible on your solo policy was $5,000, you could save $2,600. The money does not need to be spent each calendar year; it can roll over from year to year until used.

Your employer may offer the HSA in conjunction with a High Deductible Health Plan, and may even contribute to it on your behalf. Check with your HR department. If you need to go outside your company to set up an account, first check to see if the company providing your health insurance offers these accounts. Health insurers such as UniCare, Fortis, Blue Cross Blue Shield and Golden Rule currently offer HSAs. (Or go to www.hsainsider.com to locate an insurer in your state.) You might also check with your bank, broker or credit union.

Note: If you open an HSA, hold onto your receipts in case the IRS ever wants proof that you did, in fact, spend the money on medical expenses.

## Disability Insurance

If you have a job with good benefits, your employer probably provides you with short- and long-term disability coverage. Employer-sponsored short-term disability (STD) usually covers 50 percent to 60 percent of weekly salary up to twenty-six weeks (depending on your company's policies and the laws in some states) if you miss work due to a non-work-related illness (e.g., pregnancy). Of course, your employer could opt to replace your full salary for some or all of that time.

Long-term disability (LTD), which is not required by any laws, kicks in if an illness or injury causes you to miss work for an extended period of time. These plans usually cover 50 percent to 60 percent of your monthly salary and go into effect after STD has been exhausted. Usually the employer pays the full premium. Some employers allow you to buy additional LTD insurance, so that your income could be further supplemented, up to 70 percent. Insurers don't offer policies providing full salary replacement, since they want you to stay motivated to get better and return to work.

For many people, disability is a 60/90/120 day event, notes Greg McGraime, CFP and vice president at JPMorgan Chase Bank in New York City. If you don't have STD from work replacing your income, it's unlikely that you're going to purchase it yourself—it's prohibitively expensive. That's why it's important to have an adequate emergency fund to cover living expenses for four to six months in case, among other things, you find yourself temporarily out of commission.

LTD is another matter. The idea is to protect your income over a long period of time, for anywhere from one year to fifty years or more, if you are unable to earn it yourself. For many couples who are not covered by LTD at work, buying a policy is about number ten on their list of top ten priorities (if it even makes the list)! But financial planners believe that's a big mistake. "If you became disabled at age twenty-five, you would have years of financial support needs ahead of you," says McGraime. Think about it: If you became unable to perform your job and lost your salary, would your DH be able to earn enough to maintain your home and standard of living, particularly if you had already started a family? And what if your DH were physically unable to work? Suppose he couldn't leave the house and needed home health care? Could your salary alone cover the mortgage and all other expenses for the next fifty-plus years? What if you were raising children as well?

Admittedly, pondering such scenarios has about as much appeal as sitting in three hours of traffic at the end of a holiday weekend. But let's say you're willing to explore the possibility of taking out policies for you and your DH. What should you look for and what can you do to control the cost? Ask yourself these questions about any policy you consider:

- *When do payments begin?* The longer you wait to receive benefits, the lower the premium. You could choose to wait for 60, 90 or even 180 days before collecting any salary replacement. Of course the longer you wait, the more you will need an alternate source of funds to replace income during that time. On top of that, the first check usually isn't paid until 30 days past the waiting period.

- *For how long will I be covered?* It could be one year, five years, to age sixty-five or for your lifetime. The less time you're covered, the lower the premium. However, if you need this insurance at all it's not so much for the two-month disability but the one that takes you permanently out of the workforce. What you're looking for, then, is a policy that provides coverage until age sixty-five. Another feature to consider adding is an inflation option; each year your benefit would increase by, say, 5 percent, to keep pace with inflation. It's also possible to add a cost-of-living adjustment, but this doesn't kick in until you've been disabled for a year.

- *Is there a waiver of premium provision?* This would allow you to stop paying premiums after you're disabled for ninety days (a good idea since you would be living on less income). It should be included in the premium quoted.

- *How much will I receive?* Most likely you will be limited to 70 to 80 percent of your monthly income from all sources, including Social Security, if you also qualify to receive a disability benefit from the government. Again, the idea is to motivate you to go back to work and replace your full salary.

- *How is disability defined?* You'll really want to nail down how your insurer defines *disabled*. Some pay benefits if you can't perform the duties of your customary occupation, while others only pay if you're unable to perform any job that's suitable, based on your education and experience. The most prevalent policies cover you as long as you can't perform the duties of your occupation, as long as you're not working at some other occupation. The best policy would cover you in your occupation until you reach age sixty-five, even if you're working in another occupation (paying you benefits but also allowing you to earn some income).

- *Source of disability?* You want a policy to cover you for both accidents and illness. Some only cover for accidents. It's not enough, especially as you get older. Top causes of disability aren't debilitating accidents, but osteoarthritis, back pain, heart disease, respiratory conditions and cancer, notes Carol Harnett, a group disability expert with Hartford Financial Services Group in Hartford, Connecticut.

- *Are residual benefits included?* If you're not totally disabled, this would allow you to return to work part-time and still receive a partial payment based on your loss of income.

- *Is presumptive disability included?* This means that even if you could do some or all of your job, you are considered disabled and entitled to full benefits if you've lost your sight, hearing, speech or use of limbs.

- *Is it noncancelable?* Some policies are noncancelable, which means the company can't raise your premiums or cancel you as long as you keep paying the premiums. Others are guaranteed renewable. You can renew, but the company has the right to raise your premium as long as it raises everybody else's in the same rating class as you.

- *How healthy is the insurance company?* Before you sign on any dotted line, check out the company at A.M. Best (www.ambest .com). You want to be sure the company is sound and will be around if you ever need it to pay up. Look for a rating of A++ or A+.

## General Tips for Saving on Insurance Costs

- As if I need to say it: Don't smoke! You'll pay not only in the health risks you take, but in higher premiums not only for life insurance, but for nongroup medical, car and homeowner's insurance. And at $4 a pack, who needs it?

- Increase the deductibles and don't file small claims. It's ironic (since you're paying for the coverage!) but filing small claims or even making inquiries about claims could result in a premium hike. Lost your digital camera? Best to fughedaboutit, from an insurance point-of-view.

- Comparison shop. Premiums can vary greatly; just make sure you're comparing apples to apples when looking at plans. Also shop the policy when it's time to renew. Don't feel wedded to your insurer. If you can find a better deal, take it.

- Buy more than one policy from your insurance company. Usually you can get a price break if you buy multiple policies, such as car and homeowner's/renter's.

- Ask your insurer if there are any discounts available. For example, taking a safe driving course could cut you a small break on your auto insurance.

- Always check to see if you can buy from a group plan, such as a professional, business or alumni group to which you may belong. There is a good chance the rates will be less than what you can find elsewhere. Note: Some insurances are offered as part of a cafeteria-style benefits plan at work, so be sure to review your benefits before shopping elsewhere. If, for example, disability is offered at work, that is the place to get it, even if you have to kick in some from your paycheck. You won't find a better deal elsewhere. For example, a group long-term disability policy with Hartford Financial Services Group would only cost about $180 per year to insure 60 percent of your income.

- Maintain your credit rating. It is looked at when you apply for car and homeowner's insurance and can affect your premiums. Why should your credit history matter? Because the insurance industry has picked up on the fact that people with good credit histories have fewer accidents.

## Car Insurance

Most likely you and your DH already have your own cars and insurance. Still, postwedding is a good time to review your policies; you might be able to save some bucks by putting more than one car on a policy. Be sure to shop around. You could start by considering what each of your current insurers could offer now that you're married and insuring two cars, but also consider whether you could get a better deal with a new insurer.

Just to review Car Insurance 101, the main factors in keeping costs down are your driving record, the type of car and number of miles you drive and the number of claims you have filed in the past. While we're in review mode, here's what to focus on when considering new policies, according to the Insurance Information Institute:

1. *Bodily injury liability.* This covers injuries that you, the policy-holder or the driver causes to someone else. It's important to have an adequate amount of this type of insurance to protect assets such as your home and investments. If you are in a serious accident, you could be sued for a great deal of money. This is also a reason to have an umbrella liability policy. Such a policy kicks in once you reach the liability coverage on your car insurance. Insurance companies typically want you to have at least $250,000 of liability coverage before they'll sell you an umbrella policy—and fortunately, they're affordable. You could get a $1 million personal umbrella liability policy for about $150 to $300 per year. Even if you don't have assets that someone could go after, there are always your wages that could be garnished. Given the litigious society we live in, it could be worth it to have the additional coverage.

2. *Medical payments, or Personal Injury Protection (PIP).* This pays for treatment of injuries to the driver and passengers in your car.

3. *Property damage liability.* This pays for damage that you (or someone driving your car with permission) causes to someone else's property, typically their car.

4. *Collision.* This pays for the damage to your car as the result of an accident, whether or not you are at fault. You probably don't need collision insurance on an older car that isn't worth much. If the car is wrecked you won't get much of anything back anyway. If you need collision insurance, you can lower the premium by increasing the deductible.

5. *Comprehensive.* This covers you if your car is stolen or if it's damaged by something other than a car accident, such as an earthquake, hurricane, riot, vandalism, fire, missiles, explosion or running into an animal like a deer. The deductible on

comprehensive is usually $100 to $300. As with collision, opt for a higher deductible and you can lower the premium.

6. *Uninsured and underinsured motorist coverage.* This coverage allows you to collect for damages to your car and for your injuries (and those of any passengers) if you can't collect from the driver who hit you because he or she is uninsured or underinsured. This form of protection, required in some states, also provides coverage if you are hit by a hit-and-run driver.

## Life Insurance

Until you start a family, you probably don't have a massive need for life insurance. However, here are some situations in which a life insurance policy would make sense for you and your DH:

- You've bought a house each of you would want to stay in but couldn't afford on your own.

- You have considerable bills to pay off—credit cards, student loans, car loans.

- One or both of you would need financial help in the absence of one of your incomes for getting on your feet—for example, help paying the mortgage while trying to sell the house, or money to complete school or get an advanced degree.

Obviously, once you have a baby, both of you absolutely must have an adequate life insurance policy to cover the cost of raising the child (or children) solo through college, if necessary. As an example, the policy amount might be five to eight times your current income. But let's consider what you need to meet current needs.

## How Much Insurance Should I Get?

In having a discussion about the size of your policies, consider all of your debts, including the mortgage, if there is one, along with anything else you would want to take care of. The basic question to ask is, If I died tomorrow, how much would you need to get by for what period of time, also allowing for a grieving period? Consider all of your debts, education and any other needs, as well as funeral expenses (average cost of basic funeral and burial is $7,000 to $10,000). The good news is that because you are young and presumably healthy, life insurance will be quite affordable, depending on the type you get.

## Okay, What Type of Insurance Should I Get?

Here's the short answer: Buy term insurance. Most money pros believe that life insurance should simply provide death protection—and that's exactly what term insurance does. Unlike other types of insurance, term insurance doesn't have any savings/investing component to it—and that's okay. The way it works is if you should die, your beneficiary receives the full face value of the policy, and the money is paid tax-free. Because you are young and healthy (partial definition of healthy: you don't smoke!) you and your DH could each pick up a level premium twenty-year policy very inexpensively. For example, a twenty-nine-year-old nonsmoking woman in excellent health could purchase a $250,000 twenty-year level premium term policy for $175 per year, or about $15 a month, from TIAA-CREF Life Insurance Company, a top-rated insurer. They're practically giving it away! Wait another ten or twenty years and the annual premium could be ten times that—and that is precisely why you should get a policy and lock in a rate while you're in your twenties. Here's a breakdown of the various available options.

## TERM

As mentioned, you buy a policy that pays a death benefit over a specified period of time, anywhere from one to thirty years. If you die during that time, your beneficiaries collect the face value of the policy. There are differences in term policies based on renewability.

*Renewable term.* You can renew your coverage at the end of the term; a physical isn't required, but the premium will increase each time. Sometimes,when people are starting out and money is tight, they first go for a very inexpensive renewable term policy. This is a smart idea—they get the underwriting done when they are young and very healthy. The policy can then be increased—to a point—later without going through the underwriting process again (medical exam).

*Level term.* Offers a fixed premium for a set period of time, typically ten or twenty years. You don't suffer a rate increase until you renew your policy. A physical may be required at that time, depending on the insurer.

*Convertible term insurance.* This means your term insurance could be converted to a permanent policy (see below) without having to submit to a physical exam. Premiums for convertible policies are usually higher than they are for nonconvertibles. In addition, after you switch to a permanent policy the premiums will increase for the same death benefit you had when it was term policy. On the plus side—please, there has to be one!—the premiums will remain the same while the term premiums increase on renewal.

## PERMANENT

There are various types of policies called "permanent" because they last your lifetime, as long as you keep paying the premiums. They do not expire after a certain number of years, as is the case with term policies. These policies cost considerably more than term policies, and they have a savings component. The amount of the death benefit is not the same as the cash value (the cash value is that part of your premium that goes into savings or investments, and it is considerably less). The savings in these policies grows on a tax-deferred basis. You can take a loan against the cash value you've accumulated, or you can surrender the policy and walk away with the savings. Or, you can let the savings accumulate. You can also use the cash value to pay your premiums, if you have enough in your account to do so. Here are the types of permanent policies available.

*Whole life.* This is considered the most conservative of the permanent policies; it's for people who don't want any surprises. The premiums are fixed and the amount of the death benefit is guaranteed until you reach age 100. The company may pay dividends, if its investments perform well.

*Universal life.* This type of policy has a lot of flexibility built in, but what you end up with at the end of the day is not certain. With this policy, you can pay your premium at any time, in any amount, within the guidelines of certain minimums and maximums. A minimum death benefit amount is guaranteed, but the cash value you build up is not. It can be adversely affected if, for example, the insurance company decides to increase administrative expenses, or if its investments don't do well. With this policy, you can increase the death benefit as time goes on if you pass a physical exam (instead of being stuck with a death benefit fixed at the time you take out the policy). In addition, you can stop or reduce your premiums, letting the cash value you've built up pay the premium. The danger is if you can't afford the premium and there isn't enough cash value to cover the cost, your policy would then lapse and all that money you shelled out for premiums will have been for naught. The savings component in these policies pays you an interest rate—a bit better than you might get from a money market account—for example, around 4.75 percent. But the rate is not guaranteed. There are a lot of "ifs" built into permanent plans. Enter at your own risk.

*Variable life.* With this policy, you can invest your cash value in stocks, bonds and money market mutual funds, so there is the potential for earning a greater return than in policies paying interest/dividends. Of course, when you invest in the stock market you take greater risks. Your cash value and the death benefit could decrease if your investments don't do well. Some plans guarantee a minimum death benefit, no matter what.

*Variable-universal life.* A combo of the two: You can take the investment risks of the variable policy, combined with the ability to adjust the premiums and death benefit, à la the universal policy.

The argument you'll hear in favor of permanent insurance is that, well, it's permanent and the policy won't expire. But the premiums are often so expensive that people let them lapse—and then, yes, the policy does expire. The savings component is often touted as a form of retirement savings. But the sales commissions you pay are considerable, and the cash value is never as high as you think it will be. It's better to save for retirement not through an insurance company, but by investing in mutual funds via IRAs, 401(k)s and other savings vehicles you can track and which offer you more control over what you're actually investing in. "It's cheaper and easier to save outside an insurance policy," says Bonnie A. Hughes, CFP, founder of A & H Financial Planning and Education, Inc., in Rome, Georgia. Another common refrain among money experts is to buy term and invest the difference (of what you'd pay for a permanent policy). "But even if

## QUESTIONS TO ASK REGARDING PERMANENT POLICIES

These are not the most transparent investment products in the world to understand. That's why it's important to keep asking questions so that you understand exactly what you're getting for your money. Here are some basic questions to ask an agent:

1.  What is the death benefit? How can or does it change over time?

2.  What factors impact the cash value of the policy?

3.  What are the fees/commissions I am charged each year? What are they for? Ask the agent to translate them into dollars and cents (instead of just hearing 3 percent for one thing and 2 percent for another). Consider how much your savings would have to earn to first equal, and then surpass, the money being deducted for fees.

4.  How financially healthy is the insurer? (See below for checking this independently.)

5.  What is the company's track record on raising the cost of insurance? (Here you are trying to learn how frequently and by how much the company will increase fees.) The agent should be able to tell you if they raise fees yearly, once every ten years, never . . . and by what percentage they have historically raised fees.

6.  If you're considering variable life or variable-universal, find out where the money is invested—with which mutual funds? Check Morningstar (www.morningstar.com) for the performance of the funds.

7.  Ask what optional benefits come with the contract (e.g., for long-term care), when you can buy them and what they would cost. You don't need long-term care insurance now, but you will in twenty years or so.

8.  How is the death benefit paid? Is it a lump sum? Could it be paid out over a number of years?

you don't invest the difference it's hard to justify the expense of whole life," says Hughes.

## Where to Buy Life Insurance

There are three basics ways to buy:

1. Through your company. Employers sometimes provide a term policy, which could be up to five times your salary, depending on what you earn. Usually the company-provided coverage isn't enough. Find out what it would cost for you to increase your coverage, but don't assume this source will give you the best deal. Before you buy at work, compare the price of term policies elsewhere.

2. Through an insurance agent. You could contact any major insurance company for help in selecting a policy and determining the correct amount of coverage, but don't feel pressured into buying a policy you don't understand or don't feel you need.

3. Online. Check out sites such as www.einsurance.com, where you can get a quote, find an agent and get questions answered. Consider low-load companies that sell life insurance at low or no commission. Two to try include Ameritas (www.ameritas.com) 1-800-745-1112 or USAA Life Insurance Company at 1-800-531-8000 (skip their website; you need to be a member to get information).

When shopping for a life insurance policy, always be sure to check the health and financial strength of the company before you sign on—you want to be sure it'll be around to pay up, if need be. You can check the ratings at sites such as A.M. Best (www.ambest.com). Only deal with companies that earn top ratings, such as A++ and A+. In addition, if you can afford to make your payments once a year, do so. You can opt for monthly or semiannual payments, but the premiums will be higher, especially if you go monthly.

## When to Review Your Policy

You should review coverage each year, but the following events are definite triggers for taking another look. You may need to increase your policy, or you may discover you no longer need as much:

- Birth or adoption of a child

- Inheritance received

- Your money situation changes substantially—either an increase or decrease in salary

- Major increase in debt/buy a house

- Divorce

## Homeowner's/Renter's Insurance

If you buy a house, you'll need to have homeowner's insurance (it's not required by law, but your lender will require it). Even if it weren't required, you would certainly want insurance to protect your investment. On the other hand, nobody forces you to buy renter's insurance, but if you rent, you should have it. Your landlord's property insurance does not cover the contents of your apartment. If a fire swept through your complex or you were robbed, could you afford to replace all of your most valuable possessions? Probably not, which is why renter's insurance is a necessity.

## Homeowner's: What You Need to Know

The most important factor in buying a homeowner's policy is to get the proper amount of coverage. The average cost for homeowner's insurance in 2004 was approximately $608, according to the Insurance Information Institute, although rates vary significantly, depending on where you live and the type of house you own. You'll want to get **comprehensive coverage** that insures both your house and its contents. Given the many natural disasters of late—hurricanes in Florida, wildfires in California—there has been much discussion about homeowners being underinsured. When your insurance is not enough to cover your losses, you face not having adequate funds to rebuild, coupled with still having a mortgage to pay off. According to Marshall & Swift/Boeckh, a company that helps insurers determine the value of houses, 64 percent of homes are underinsured by an average of 27 percent. Some are underinsured by 60 percent or more.

It used to be that homeowners could buy a policy that would cover the rebuilding of their home if it were destroyed, no matter the cost to the insurer. But that has been replaced by something called an **extended replacement policy**, which pays the amount stated on the policy (for example, $150,000), plus another 20 to 25 percent. Ideally what you want is called a **guaranteed replacement cost policy**. Obviously premiums on such a policy will be higher, typically by 20 to 25 percent. But such complete coverage isn't readily available. Only a few companies sell it, and usually for homes worth $500,000 or more.

What can you do to adequately protect your home? For starters, when buying a policy get a second opinion on how much coverage you actually need. You can find out what it would cost to rebuild your house by getting an estimate from a contractor or a public claims adjuster (typically you hire them to negotiate a settlement with an insurance company over a sizeable property loss). Second, review your policy each year and keep it up to date. Increase your coverage whenever you make improvements to your home, such as remodeling or adding another room.

Insurers also advise buying inflation-guard endorsements on their policies, which only cost a few dollars a month. This added protection automatically adjusts how much insurance you buy each year to keep up with increases in local building costs. According to the Insurance Information Institute, if you bought a home ten years ago with an insured value of $100,000, it would cost $134,000 to rebuild it today, assuming a 3 percent inflation rate in repair and rebuilding costs. It's important when you think about this type of insurance to not just think of what your house is worth right now, but what it would cost to rebuild it in today's dollars. That's the coverage amount you want to keep pace with.

If you live in an area prone to earthquakes or flooding, you'll need additional coverage for that. Ditto for other valuables such as jewelry (your engagement ring, etc.), fine art, coin or stamp collections and camera and computer equipment. In terms of your other possessions (clothes, furniture, etc.) you'll want to get a **replacement cost policy** rather than **actual cash value coverage**. With a replacement cost policy the insurer will pay to replace your belongings with similar, new items. With actual cash value coverage, you're reimbursed for what the item is worth now. So if your ten-year-old stereo system is destroyed in a fire, with actual cash value coverage you would get what you would expect to pay for a ten-year-old stereo system. With a replacement cost policy, you get a new stereo system with similar features to your old one.

Homeowner's insurance also includes personal liability coverage, which covers accidents such as someone tripping on your steps and breaking his arm. We had earlier talked about purchasing an umbrella policy for $1 million. This would supplement the liability coverage in your homeowner's policy—a good idea in today's litigious world.

## Keeping Good Records

You'll need to keep a record of your belongings for insurance purposes. My husband and I keep a list of our stuff in an Excel spread
sheet, which can easily be printed out and stashed in our safe deposit
box. By keeping the list in the computer, we can easily update it. However you choose to do this, you'll need to list each item, the brand
name and model number, a general description, the date and cost
when purchased (or an estimate) and what it would cost to replace it.
It's also a good idea to walk around the house/apartment/garage with
a video camera and tape all of your belongings, or walk around and
take pictures of everything. These records should be kept in a safe
place such as a safe deposit box. Since you have provided the cost/es-
timate for each item, along with the cost of replacement you can now
add everything up and have a good idea of how much your insurance
coverage should be for personal possessions.

## Controlling the Cost

Here, according to the Insurance Information Institute, are top ways
to save money on your homeowner's insurance:

1. Raise the deductible. A deductible of at least $500 is recom-
   mended, but if you raise it to $1,000, you could save up to 25
   percent. Going with a higher deductible makes sense anyway,
   since insurers consider it a strike against you when you file
   small claims.

2. Don't include the value of your land when insuring your house.
   The land can't be stolen, or swept away in a tornado, etc.

3. Ask what improvements/additions you can make to earn discounts. For example, if you installed smoke detectors (which

you should have anyway), or a burglar alarm, how much money would you save?

4. Buy your car insurance from the same company. The insurer may knock 5 to 15 percent off your premium if you have more than one policy with them.

5. Maintain a good credit record. Insurers these days are using your credit information to price car and homeowner's policies—just another reason to pay your bills on time and check your credit record for mistakes once a year.

## Renter's: What You Need to Know

Your renter's insurance reimburses you for property destroyed in case of things like fire, or if your bed gets hit by lightning and goes up in flames (that happened to my mother—fortunately not while she was in it!), if someone breaks in and steals your computer or if a volcano erupts, covering your stuff with ash. You get the picture. Of the seventeen basic types of "perils" covered under a basic policy, floods and earthquakes aren't included, so you would have to get a rider covering those natural disasters.

In terms of the type of insurance to get, you'll want to follow the same guidelines as homeowner's, where protection of your possessions is concerned. You want **replacement cost coverage** for your belongings, not actual cash value. With replacement cost coverage, you will be paid what it costs to replace the item, up to the limit stated in your policy (be sure to ask what those limits are, so there aren't any surprises later). With actual cash value, you're paid what the item is worth. So if your five-year-old $300 TV set is ruined when your upstairs neighbor's bathtub overflows, pouring water onto your set, you would get, what, $50, or whatever a five-year-old TV set is worth.

You'll probably need to buy a separate rider for valuables such as jewelry (your bling), computer and other electronic equipment, any antiques, furs, etc. Be sure to tell the insurance agent what you've got so he or she can advise you about purchasing adequate coverage for these more expensive items.

You'll also need to make an inventory of your belongings and keep that list in a safe place. For further instruction see "Keeping Good Records" in the Homeowner's Insurance section.

Usually renter's policies cover your living expenses (up to a point) if something happens in your apartment to make it uninhabitable (we're talking events like a fire, not a fight with your DH). Be sure to find out how much you're insured for living elsewhere while your home is repaired, or until you relocate. Typically the coverage is limited to 30 to 40 percent of the total value of the policy. For example, if you're insured for $75,000, you would receive $22,500 or $30,000 for additional living expenses, per the terms of your policy.

Finally, renter's insurance will give you some liability coverage. So if someone trips on your living room rug, somersaults over the coffee table and lands with a thud on their head, spraining their neck, you would be covered for medical costs, up to your liability limit. You would also be covered up to your policy's limit if you are sued and they win a judgement against you.

Here are a few tried-and-true ways to reduce the cost of renter's insurance:

- Buy your car insurance with the same company.

- Increase the deductible, if you can afford to do so.

- Ask about discounts if you install smoke or fire detectors or burglar alarms.

## A Final Word About Insurance

Insurance: It is boring. But insurance covering the various aspects of our lives is also one of the cornerstones for building financial security in our society. Without it, you could end up in a financial wipeout that could take years from which to recover. That's not how you want to spend your prime earning years—you want to spend them accumulating assets that will appreciate over time. When reviewing any of the policies you're presented with, ask questions so that you understand the coverage you are getting. Ask the agent "what if " questions addressing your biggest concerns. You certainly don't want to spend unnecessarily on premiums, but you also don't want to be penny-wise and pound-foolish. Get enough coverage to protect you and your DH in case something really unpleasant happens in terms of your health, your car, your home, your life. At the least you should sleep better at night, knowing you've covered your ASSets.

# 11. Marriage: It's Taxing

The first thing—taxwise, anyway—you and your DH should do post-marriage is a rough estimate of what your tax bill will be as a married couple. Then, adjust your withholding, if necessary, so that you don't have too much or too little taken out of your paychecks. Ideally you'll net out at zero on April 15, not owing taxes and not getting a refund check, which is money you could have been using throughout the year had it not been withheld. See chapter 4 for specific steps on how to review your withholding.

## The Marriage Penalty

You've undoubtedly heard about the marriage penalty. What is the marriage penalty, anyway? It refers to the fact that (historically) you and your spouse, with your combined incomes, would pay more in tax than you would as two singles. Example: Let's say that you and your DH each earn $70,350. As two singles, that would put you each in the 25 percent tax bracket (for a total of $140,700 of taxable income). Let's say, however, that the two of you are married. All of a sudden, with a *combined* taxable income of $140,700, you are now in the 28 percent tax bracket. As a married couple, you couldn't earn more than $117,250 before you shoot up to the next tax bracket.

Some changes were made in the tax law in 2003 to eliminate the penalty for those taxpayers in lower income brackets. Those changes were set to expire, and at press time it remains to be seen whether or not they will be extended.

And now for some riveting back story: The marriage penalty isn't something that was intentionally dreamed up by the government to go after married couples. In fact, up until 1969, singles paid more in taxes than married couples did. That was changed, reports the Tax Foundation, when an unmarried activist named Vivien Kellerns and her allies lobbied Congress for changes in the tax law, eliminating the disparity, and won—except the balance of who was paying more then tipped in favor of marrieds. The problem is that there are so many provisions in the code—some of which favor marrieds and some of which favor singles—that it's extremely difficult to get it to come out even without hurting some group. The foundation further notes that the main culprits that keep the marriage penalty alive are the standard deduction and the nature of income tax brackets. What does that mean? In 2004, for example, the standard deduction for married filers was $9,500, or exactly twice (200 percent) that of single filer's deduction, which was $4,750. That's fair. But in the past, married couples didn't get a standard deduction equal to what two single people got; they got less. For example, a married couples' deduction might have been only 174 percent that of single filers. So if a single got a deduction of $4,750, a married couple only got a deduction of $8,265 (174 percent) instead of $9,500. (The thinking was that two live more cheaply than one, and it all washed out in the end.) What about the tax brackets? There has been a similar problem. Married taxpayers typically found that their joint income was taxed at higher rates. In addition, combining incomes typically pushes couples into higher tax brackets. Tax laws will continue to change, of course, over your lifetime. You may have a respite from the marriage penalty now, but it may turn up again later.

There are other ways in which combining your income through marriage can have a negative impact on your taxes. This is especially true when someone with a low income marries someone with a high income: The lower earner may find that he or she no longer qualifies for certain tax credits that phase out as income increases. Let's say, for example, that you earn $40,000 per year. Under the tax code, you could deduct the interest paid on a student loan as long as your modified adjusted gross income doesn't exceed $50,000. But then you marry someone who earns $100,000. Your household income is now $140,000. At that income level you exceed the limit and lose the deduction. (By the way, you would have to file Married Filing Jointly to claim this deduction, if you still qualified for it.) Speaking of which . . .

## Should I File Married Filing Jointly or Married Filing Separately?

You have two choices for filing after you marry: Married Filing Jointly and Married Filing Separately. Your marital status on the last day of the year determines how you file. That means if you are single on December 31, you file as a single. If you marry on December 31, you file married (jointly or separate), even though you were only married for one day of the year. That's why couples who want to marry near year's end sometimes wait until January, if it could save them several thousand dollars in additional taxes (hey, enough for a hot honeymoon). If you are considering a December wedding, check with your accountant to see how much it will cost you.

According to Marsha G. LePhew, a CPA in Rock Hill, South Carolina, it usually makes sense for married couples to file a joint return. There are just a few incidents when you might consider filing separately:

1. If you have any concerns about what your spouse reports on his return (for example, deductions taken or amount of income reported). If you file jointly and sign the return, you are vouching for its veracity. If there are problems down the line, you will be equally responsible for them.

2. If one of you has a large amount of employee business expenses that are eligible for deduction. In order to take the deduction, the business expenses incurred need to be over 2 percent of your adjusted gross income. If you combine your income with your spouse's on a joint return, your expenses may no longer meet that threshold and you would lose out on the deduction. If your business expenses are sizeable, ask your accountant about filing separate returns. Note that this rule does not impact your situation if one or both of you is self-employed. In that situation, you would be filing a Schedule C and deducting your expenses on it.

3. If one of you has considerable medical expenses. You can deduct medical expenses that exceed 7.5 percent of your AGI. Again, it's possible that by combining incomes your expenses would no longer make that threshold, causing you to lose the deduction.

If you are considering filing separate returns, calculate your tax both ways. Sometimes you end up owing more by going the separate route. Your income may hit the upper tax brackets sooner than a single taxpayer would. For example, using 2004 tax rates, if you earn $60,000 and file married separate, you would be in the 28 percent tax bracket. If you were single, you would be in the 25 percent bracket.

Note: If you file "Married Separate" and your spouse itemizes, you need to itemize, too.

Tax breaks you lose by filing Married Filing Separately:

- You can't deduct interest paid on a qualified student loan or claim the tuition and fees deduction.

- You can't deduct your contributions to an IRA and you're not allowed to contribute to a Roth IRA if your modified adjusted gross income (MAGI) is $10,000 or more.

- You can't claim education credits, such as the Hope or the Lifetime Learning Credit.

If nothing else, filing jointly means one less return to prepare and file. Only go the separate route if there is a compelling reason to do so.

## Tax Breaks: Yeah Right

Well, how does a middle-class person get a tax break these days? Unfortunately there aren't that many. The main deductions are mortgage interest and property taxes for homeowners, state income tax, IRA deductions, if you qualify, and education deductions, as mentioned above. Also, don't overlook opportunities through your employer to defer taxes through contributions to retirement plans or to reduce taxes by taking advantage of medical spending accounts.

# 12. Estate Planning: Do It Now, While You Still Think You'll Live Forever!

You may think you don't really need a will yet. You may think you're too young, or that you don't have enough assets to worry about. That's understandable. That's the way I thought for a long time, even though it sometimes bothered me late at night that I hadn't taken care of this (which was insane, actually, since I was a single mother for several years).

Here's what one bride had to say on the subject, which was fairly typical: "We haven't talked about wills/living wills, etc., extensively. I know that my husband has some life insurance and that I am named as beneficiary. He is the beneficiary on my work-provided life insurance plan. This is something we need to discuss further, but we're young and we just got married!" Another common remark: "Once we bought our house, we knew we should get life insurance. So now we have life insurance. Once we have children, then we'll talk about a will."

These attitudes could, unfortunately, result in a complicated and messy financial situation, on top of the heartache, if the unthinkable were to occur (which is part of the reason we don't think about it).

The fact is that everyone needs a will—even if you're young, just starting out, and don't yet have children. If you die without one, it's called *intestate*. The state you live in then supplies you with a will according to its laws (so there's no getting around having a will, one way or another) and chances are you won't like what the state provides. For example, in New Jersey, if you die without a will, are married and your parents are still alive, your spouse would only get a portion of your assets—and your parents would get the balance, points out Warren Racusin, senior estate planning partner with McElroy, Deutsch, Mulvaney & Carpenter in Morristown, New Jersey. Racusin's firm, which represents a number of families of September 11 victims, has seen this problem quite a bit. "Parents are entitled to a lot of the assets," he says. As another example, in Connecticut a

## CHOOSING AN ATTORNEY

It is important to select an estate attorney who will not only be knowledgeable about your state's laws but who is also familiar with drafting wills, probate and estate and inheritance tax planning. When interviewing prospective attorneys, ask how many wills they have written and how many estates they have administered. For a simple will a young attorney could be the most cost-effective choice. But if your estate is in any way complicated, you'll want an attorney who has been practicing for at least a few years. In addition, find out which organizations they belong to, such as the probate section of their local bar association, or the American College of Trust and Estate Counsel. Once you've met with a lawyer and you've agreed to work together, he or she should give you a letter stating what the fees are for preparing the will along with other necessary documents, such as a living will and power of attorney and, if appropriate, a living trust.

surviving spouse would be entitled to the first $100,000 and three-quarters of the remainder of an estate, with the deceased's parents receiving the other one-quarter.

Hopefully this has opened your eyes enough that you will immediately ask relatives, friends and other professionals in your life, such as your accountant, for their recommendations of estate lawyers. You could also jump-start your search online, at the site of the Martindale-Hubbell Law Directory (www.martindale.com). The site allows you to search for a lawyer by specialty. It then provides contact and biographical information, such as where the lawyer went to school, the type of law practiced and a link to the firm's website. The site also rates attorneys from A to C (A being the highest), using opinions solicited from other lawyers and judges. Another site to check out is that of the American College of Trust and Estate Counsel (www.actec.org). This is an invitation-only membership group of top estate lawyers across the country.

## What Does It Cost?

The cost of a will depends on where you live and how complicated your situation is. Estimates for a simple will would run from about $500 to $1,000. You and your DH can use the same lawyer—but if you do use the same lawyer, he or she can't "keep" anything from your spouse. Not that you would want to anyway. (Fun fact: It's illegal to disinherit your beloved. A spouse is entitled to a minimum of your estate, ranging from one-third to one-half, depending on which state you live in.)

There is also, of course, will-making software available. You could certainly save a few bucks by going this route, but since laws vary by state, why take the risk that something could be overlooked or not drawn up properly? If and when you start a family, you would need to revise your will and would certainly want an attorney reviewing that version. Perhaps best to start the process with a professional to begin with.

After you've selected an attorney, he or she will probably give you an informational sheet to fill out before your first meeting. You'll use this to list all of your assets, their value and how your assets are titled (whose name they're in), such as your cars and home. You'll also be asked to list your debts. You'll then take this to your first appointment and review it, discussing what you would want to have happen with various assets should you die. It goes without saying that you will likely leave the bulk of your estate to your spouse, although you may want to bequeath certain special items to individuals, such as a piece of jewelry to a sister or best friend, or some token amount to a favorite charity.

Lawyers try to cover all of the bases when writing wills so that you don't have to constantly update it. They create scenarios such as, if your spouse predeceases you and you inherit his assets, how would you want to disburse them if you then die? Or what happens if you die together? After you've gone over the various scenarios and outlined how you would want your assets distributed, the lawyer prepares a draft for each of you for review.

## Naming an Executor

One of the things you will do in having your will drafted is to name an executor. An executor is the person who settles your affairs should you die. You will very likely name your spouse as executor, and he you. But you each need a backup as well, called a *successor executor*.

Functioning as executor is a job. When you name your backup, you'll want to name someone with financial integrity. This person will have access to your funds, and it is up to him or her to make sure your last wishes are carried out. The executor should also have some financial competency, as he or she could be making important decisions about things like selling your house or stock portfolio. Your backup could be a relative, close friend or even your accountant.

Don't worry if the person who you feel is best suited for the job is not geographically nearby; a lot can be handled via fax and overnight mail. In a nutshell, the job of the executor is to:

- Probate the will in surrogate court (more on that later).

- Pay off your debts: Send checks to your credit card companies, pay off the car loan, etc.

- File your final income tax return.

- Collect and distribute the assets according to your will. For example, if you've left a piece of jewelry to your niece, it's the executor's job to identify the piece of jewelry and make sure she gets it.

If you're worried that your successor executor would be weighed down with a thankless job, take heart. It's actually not that complicated and the executor does collect a commission, which is determined by state law, for his or her trouble. The commission is a percentage of your assets, *excluding* the proceeds of any life insurance policy proceeds going to your spouse. For example, in New Jersey the commission is 5 percent of the first $200,000 ($10,000), 3.5 percent of the next $800,000 ($28,000), and 2 percent of everything over $1 million. When a close family member performs this function, they usually take little or no compensation.

## What Is Probate?

Every will goes through probate. It is the process by which a court verifies that a will is genuine and assigns someone to administer your estate. If you have named an executor, the court signs off on that person to settle your affairs. If you haven't named an executor, the court chooses someone—usually a family member—whom you may or may not have picked yourself. Each state has procedures that the executor must follow for the proper closing of your estate—that is, getting the debts paid, filing an income tax return and gathering and distributing your property and assets. Note: There are certain assets that avoid probate and pass directly to your named beneficiaries: For example, life insurance proceeds, IRAs, 401(k) monies and certain individually held bank accounts (if they are designated "payable on death").

## Living Trust

A revocable trust, or living trust as it's also called, functions as a substitute for, or in addition to, a will. With a living trust, assets are transferred to the trust and are managed by a trustee (which would likely be you). Should you die, the assets are distributed to your beneficiaries as you've set out in the trust. Unlike a will, a living trust does not go through probate—so your heirs could gain access to whatever they are inheriting more quickly. In addition, when a will is probated it becomes part of the public court record; a trust does not go through this process so that privacy is maintained.

Even if you have a revocable trust you would need a will to cover those assets or property that you fail/forget/neglect to put into the trust. Your attorney will advise you as to whether you need a living trust or not. (Note: Setting up and administering a living trust is more expensive to produce than a will.) According to estate attorney Warren Racusin, a couple of primary reasons why a young couple might require a revocable trust would be because they live in a state where the probate process is highly time-consuming and intrusive, such as Florida, or if family relations are such that there might be a fight over the estate. "A revocable trust can be more difficult to challenge than a will," notes Racusin.

Revocable trusts are also common if there are children from a first marriage, to insure that the children are provided for along with the surviving spouse. Revocable trusts also tend to be used by the wealthy as part of tax planning.

## Tax Planning for the Rest of Us

Each person is entitled to an exemption from federal taxes of up to $1.5 million in 2005. (The exempted amount then increases over the next few years.) But husbands and wives can leave each other unlimited property tax-free, as long as the spouse is a U.S. citizen. This includes the proceeds of your life insurance policy, your 401(k), your pension, money in your savings or other investment accounts—everything. And it passes free from federal taxes whether you have a will or not. Some states impose a state estate tax, but the rate depends on who inherits. It's typically low to nothing when a spouse or other close relative is bequeathed assets. A good estate attorney should write a will with flexibility built in so that as your estate grows over time, the will can adapt and protect your assets from taxes. Remember that assets going to a beneficiary who is not your spouse (your parents or brother or sister, or future children) could generate a federal or state estate tax. The job of the estate attorney is to protect your assets through the use of the will.

## Second Marriages and Blended Families

Warren: Is there a blanket statement that can be about the special need for wills, etc. if there are children from a first marriage—to insure that children from a first marriage are provided for, along with the new spouse. Do people in second marriages tend to get a Living Trust? Also, what about addressing guardianship of minor children? Wouldn't that be covered in the custody agreement?

## Last Wishes

You and your DH might consider writing a simple letter of instruction stating some personal final preferences (or at least tell each other, or tell your lawyer). For example, in the event that anything should happen, would you want to be buried or cremated? Is there a family burial plot? In addition, consider attaching a list of names and numbers of people to be notified, beyond the obvious. During a difficult time, would your DH have the presence of mind to locate your old college roommate's contact information? Your DH, of course, should provide the same information for you.

Once your will is finalized, you should feel a sense of relief and accomplishment for having tackled this less-than-pleasant task. Now you can file the document away and forget about it. Where to keep the original? Warren Racusin recommends that his clients keep a copy (Note: a *copy*) with their other important papers, but that they leave the original in his office. That way, it can't get lost, and clients won't be tempted to change the will by marking it up. "In New Jersey, that could revoke the entire will," he notes. Of course you can change your will as often as you want, but you must do so by having your attorney draw up something called a codicil, which you would sign and have witnessed.

When should you update? Whenever there is a major change in your life, such as:

- You have or adopt a baby

- You get a divorce or your spouse dies

- You buy or sell a major asset, such as a home

- Your financial situation changes dramatically; for example, you receive an inheritance

The great thing about having your will drawn up is that at the same time your lawyer will assist you in executing two other extremely important documents: the power of attorney and living will.

## Name That Durable Power of Attorney

You would typically give your DH durable power of attorney. It allows him to handle your finances (i.e., your 401[k] plan, along with any accounts or investments in your name only) should you become incapacitated. Incapacitated means mentally, physically or emotionally unable to function, as determined by your doctor. If you were to become unable to handle your affairs and you did not give your spouse durable power of attorney, he would have to go to court to become your legal guardian. That takes time and money. It's best, then, to simply execute this document and have it in place.

## The Living Will: Don't Leave Home Without Signing It

"We have not discussed living wills—I know they recommend doing that, and we should really do it in the near future. I guess we haven't done it yet because no one wants to think about death—especially this soon after getting married!" So said one bride, echoing others on the subject. It is true, no one wants to think about you-know-what. But the sooner you get the living will out of the way, the better. It is a simple document to sign and have in place—and it can save an enormous amount of additional anxiety, grief and soul-searching if you were in a medical situation where a living will would be useful.

The living will allows you to state your wishes about future medical treatments you do or don't want to receive if you were unable to speak for yourself—for example, if you were to lapse into a coma or become terminally ill or injured or too sick to communicate. The living will gives you an opportunity to state which, if any, life-sustaining treatments (such as tube feeding or ventilators) you would want administered to keep you alive, even if there were no hope for your recovery or chance for regaining consciousness. You might state, for example, that if you are terminally ill you wouldn't want to be artificially fed. An added element for a newlywed bride to think about would be to state how her wishes would change if she were pregnant. For example, she might want to say that if there is no hope for her recovery and she is pregnant, she would want to be kept alive on a ventilator until the child comes to term. One issue that has been debated of late is whether or not doctors should, on the request of the wife, collect sperm from a man who is comatose and dying. A man's living will could state whether or not he would want that procedure carried out, if requested.

Your estate attorney will give you a living will document to complete, or will provide the language necessary to get the job done. You could also download the form for your state from www.partnership-forcaring.org. To learn more about the types of life-sustaining treatments you might receive, order the booklet *Advance Directives and End-of-Life Decisions* from the Partnership for Caring's website. Note that these documents also include language that expressly request treatment for relieving pain and discomfort—lest you think you would not be receiving any treatment at all! That is not the case.

In some states the living will is used to name a health care proxy, or durable medical power of attorney, as it is sometimes called. In other states you need a separate document naming this individual. This is the person whom you would entrust to carry out your wishes, as stated in the living will. The person acting as your health care proxy needs to both understand your wishes (since he or she may need to make decisions based on changes in your condition) and have the strength to act on them. Most likely you will name your DH, plus a backup, such as a parent or sibling.

This document is not only important for the health care proxy—so that he has the comfort of knowing that he is adhering to your desires—but for other family members, who might otherwise question decisions the proxy might make. (Witness the recent case of Theresa Schiavo in Florida. In 1990, at the age of 25, she suffered heart failure which led to severe brain damage, leaving her in a persistent vegetative state. Eight years later her husband—believing he would be acting on his wife's wishes—wanted to stop the artificial feeding and hydration. Her parents didn't agree and a court battle ensued, lasting several more years. Enough said about the importance of advance directives!) The living will is also useful in the event that your health care proxy is unable to carry out his function—your doctors would then follow your written directives.

Now that you've take care of business, be sure you let the right people know you've done so. Obviously your DH will know you've signed a living will and named him your health care proxy, and vice versa. You might also mention to another close relative, such as your parents, that these forms exist. Keep the original copy of the durable power of attorney, living will, and medical durable power of attorney at home with your other important papers. In addition, give a copy of the living will and medical power of attorney to your doctor. You might also stash copies of these documents in your safe deposit box.

Chances are slim that any of these documents will be needed while you're young. But having them in place, you can go about your business with the freedom of knowing that if something unexpected were to happen, you have acted proactively regarding your medical care. There should also be some relief knowing exactly what your DH would want you to do on his behalf, if he were in a medical situation requiring the use of a living will.

# A Final Thought

The vexing thing about personal finance is that it's so easy to put off taking the most basic steps. In some ways, getting our finances organized—particularly when we're doing it for the first time with another person—can seem overwhelming or, at times, just plain boring. I mean, who really wants to sit down and review two health insurance policies to figure out which is the best one? Or to assess the offerings in your company's 401(k) plan?

Still, I do hope that the prospect of making the most of your money and of creating wealth with your life partner will get you excited enough to take action and shore up those areas that may need it. While it's always fun to spend money and find bargains, there is also something to be said about watching credit card balances shrink and savings and investment accounts grow.

One of the things I've tried to point out in this book is the areas in which you, as a woman, need to take care of yourself. Beyond a doubt, marriage is a partnership and should be approached as such. But that truth doesn't change the fact that it is still important for a woman to maintain some separate savings and credit. It doesn't compromise the integrity of your marriage but allows each of you to always feel equal and empowered within the context of your relationship. That is a healthy dynamic worth working for.

If you take anything away from this book, let it be this: Don't live on credit. If you have credit card debt, pay it off. Only keep one or two cards for absolute emergencies or for convenience. Credit card debt will only ruin your best-laid financial plans. Live below your means. Save at least 10 percent of your household income. Talk about your finances with your DH and discuss where you are in meeting your goals at least once a month. When you need to make a move, do research and then act. Sometimes people don't take action because they fear making a mistake. But that in itself is a mistake. Trust yourself!

## How to Reach Me

If you would like to comment on this or for information on future projects, please visit my website at www.deborahwilburn.com.

# Index